HOW TO UNDERSTAND
THE FINANCIAL PRESS

HOW TO UNDERSTAND THE FINANCIAL PRESS

JOHN ANDREW

KOGAN
PAGE

To
HPA

First published in Great Britain in 1990 by Kogan Page Limited,
120 Pentonville Road, London N1 9JN.

Editorial packaging: Redfern Publishing Services, Kenilworth.

British Library Cataloguing in Publication Data

A CIP record for this book is available from the British Library.

ISBN 0–7494–0113–3
ISBN 0–7494–0114–1 Pbk

Typeset by the Castlefield Press Ltd, Wellingborough, Northants.

Printed and bound in Great Britain by Biddles Limited, Guildford

Acknowledgements

I wish to thank the various organisations which have furnished me with information during the course of writing this book and in particular the International Stock Exchange, Reuters, the Unit Trust Association and the Association of Investment Trust Companies.

I am most grateful to all the publishers which have allowed me to reproduce text from their pages.

Richard Northedge, Deputy City Editor of the *Daily Telegraph* and Peter Card of Midland Stockbrokers kindly agreed to undertake the task of reading the manuscript. I take this opportunity to thank them for their help and assistance, but hasten to add that all errors and omissions are mine.

Finally my thanks go to Jackie Shelford for typing the manuscript so expertly.

John Andrew
June 1990

Contents

1
Financial News

'Information means money' BC Forbes, American Publisher

Introduction

Man has always had a healthy appetite for news. The outcome of wars, social scandals and political developments are all absorbed with varying degrees of interest. Add to that the fact that we now live in an age of instant communications and it becomes quite easy to see the 'how' and 'why' money is so easily made – and lost – and examples of how this happens abound from speculation on possible takeovers to poorer than anticipated company results. This was even so in the past in the era when information spread more slowly. There will always be those who anticipate the news correctly and those who do not.

Substantial market movements in the present age are generally associated with the equity or share market as opposed to gilt-edged stock. There are, of course, very strict rules regarding acting on privileged information – insider dealing (ie acting on unpublished facts) is a criminal offence.

This book is about news on the markets and how the readers can find out from whom what is correct, when it is likely to happen, how to decipher the information and therefore whether or not to take a chance – an investment on the stock market can be risky!

Supply and demand

The object of this chapter is to analyse briefly the factors which influence a share's price in the market. In simplistic terms, as with any item, whether it is an object, a service, or financial paper, it is the interaction of supply and demand which determines its price. One of the basic laws of economics is that price tends towards the level which equates supply and demand. Economists demonstrate this by reference to a graph (see Figure 1.1).

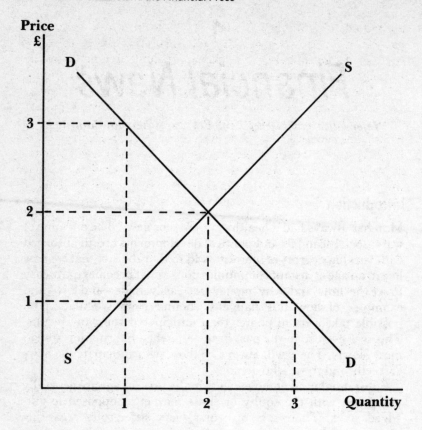

Note
DD – Demand curve
SS – Supply curve

Figure 1.1 *Demand/Supply Curve*

In basic terms, the lower the price, the greater the demand. Therefore, if an item was priced at £3, an individual may only buy one object, but if the price was reduced to £2, the same person may buy two, and if it was only £1, he may well decide to splash out and buy three of them. In graphical terms, this may be demonstrated by a line sloping downwards from left to right (see the demand curve in Figure 1.1), where the horizontal axis is quantity and the vertical axis is price. On the other hand, the individual who supplies the objects has a different behavioural pattern. If the price is high, more will be supplied than if the price was low. In graphical terms, this can be demonstrated by a line sloping upwards from left to right (see the supply curve in Figure 1.1). Should the price not be set at the point where the demand and supply curve intersect, there will either be an excess supply or demand. In a perfect world, prices will tend towards the level where demand and supply are balanced. Of course, the world is not perfect and the foregoing is a gross oversimplification of what happens in practice. However, economists all generally agree that the world's stock markets are the closest in reality to their concept of a perfect market where there is perfect competition. The assumptions upon which such a Utopian model is built are that:

- the product is homogeneous;
- there are many buyers and sellers;
- communication is perfect;
- transactions are numerous and frequent; and
- there are no barriers preventing entry to the market.

It can be appreciated why stock markets so closely reflect this theoretical concept of a perfect market. There are many buyers and sellers transacting business on a frequent basis; all the shares of a particular class in a specific company are identical; and there is an excellent communications network relaying financial information.

Communications

Quick and reliable information has always been essential to the efficient conduct of stock market business. In eighteenth-century London, business was conducted in the coffee houses of Change Alley with the waiters acting as messengers. Although internal communications were good, the market had no reliable and quick external news-gathering network. In the early nineteenth century, in an attempt to improve the situation, a number of Stock Exchange syndicates maintained pigeon lofts and operated news flights between London and Paris.

In the second half of the nineteenth century, great advances were made. First there was the telegraph, followed by the ticker-tape teleprinting machine and later the telephone. Reuters was established in 1851 and used the Dover-Calais cable to telegraph stock market quotations between London and Paris. Today Reuters is the world's leading news organisation and supplier of computerised information services. Its financial and general news is now carried by satellites, fibre optic and coaxial cables, microwave links and telephone. The *Financial Times* was also founded in the nineteenth century, with its first edition appearing in 1888. Like Reuters, it has advanced with developments in the field of communications and is now regarded as the world's leading financial newspaper.

What determines supply and demand?

Although the price of a share is determined by the interaction of supply and demand, we have to ask what determines supply and demand in order to analyse the factors which influence a share's price in the market. The glib answer is, 'anything'. Although not a very helpful response, it is nevertheless true, for the factors that influence supply and demand are all-embracing. The stock market is the barometer of the economy, so the general movement of shares reflects economic prospects. An expanding economy will attract investors and vice versa. The economic outlook is not just restricted to the UK's current or likely performance, but also to the economies of other countries. In an age where commerce knows almost no frontiers, no nation can be an island unto itself. Exchange rates are not only pertinent to those companies which export finished goods, but to the companies which import raw materials. Of course, there are factors also directly related to specific companies which can have a favourable or adverse effect on their share price. It may be a consequence of profits, or the lack of them; the development of a new product which is going to take the world by storm; the appointment of a dynamic new chairman or the resignation of a chief executive. The possibilities are endless.

Then, there are share movements that are not related to economic prospects or are not a result of news from a specific company. Investors may speculate that a company which has performed badly, with that fact being reflected in its decreased share price, will be subject to a takeover bid. The increased demand could push the share price upwards. An announcement that an airline is looking to expand its fleet could push the share prices or aircraft manufacturers generally upwards, whereas the publication of a report condemning the eating of sweets could depress the shares of companies in the confectionery industry. Then, of course, there are stockbrokers' 'buy' and 'sell' recommendations (which will be dealt with in Chapter 4), and even mere 'hunches' regarding particular shares to consider. In general terms, the factors which influence share prices may be divided into three categories:

(1) economic factors;
(2) information relating to specific companies; and
(3) miscellaneous factors.

Let us now illustrate these general points by looking at some specific cases from the latter half of 1989. Although the information is historic, the situations reflect the general factors which impact upon price movements in the equity market.

However good an individual company's news, its share price could move downwards along with a general market trend which could be following the trends on Wall Street, a result of political matters, or simply a reflection of the general outlook for the home economy.

The trade figures

The announcement of the August 1989 UK current account balance, commonly referred to as the 'trade figures', unsettled the stock market.

Shares hit as loan rates fears grow

London's financial markets took a pounding yesterday deepening fears of another rise in the cost of borrowing after the £2 billion August trade deficit announced this week. . . .

Some City analysts are convinced the Government will be forced into a politically embarassing rise of one percentage point in bank base lending rates to 15 per cent before the end of next month. . . .

A further jump in base rates would make dearer home loans almost inevitable and raise concern that the economy may be tipped into recession.

Guardian, 29 September 1989

Following this base rates *did* increase to 15 per cent.

Grey Monday

However, it was not the trade figures which had the most dramatic impact on the UK market in the autumn of 1989. One event in the US triggered a reaction through all the world's stock markets. A consortium bidding with British Airways (BA) for

United Airlines (UAL) failed to secure the required financing. Citicorp and Chase Manhattan, two of America's largest banks, were to lend US\$3bn to the consortium of UAL's managers and the pilots' union. Both banks firmly believed that they could obtain commitments from other banks to lend US\$4.2bn. When a bid is made for a company which is to be financed by borrowing it is called a leveraged buyout. The *Financial Times* reported the consequences of the failure to secure the necessary finance for the UAL buyout.

DOW FALLS 190 POINTS
COLLAPSE OF AIRLINE BUYOUT SPARKS FEARS

US stock market plunges

The US stock market yesterday suffered its steepest fall since the crash of 1987 when a plan to stage a buyout of United Airlines collapsed raising fears that banks are refusing to back debt-financed takeovers.

Minutes after management and employees at United said their lead banks had failed to syndicate the \$7.2bn (£4.5bn) in loans to finance the British Airways-backed takeover, US stock prices plunged.

The Dow Jones Industrial Average of blue-chip stocks fell 190.58 points to 2569.26, a drop of 6.91 per cent and the worst fall since the crash of October 19, 1987. Amid a wave of computerised – or programme – selling, trading in stock index futures was suspended for the first time under a 'circuit-breaker' mechanism introduced after the crash.

Financial Times, 14/15 October 1989

The speed with which the market plunged was dramatic. Just before 1500 hours, the consortium bidding for UAL announced its bankers' failure to arrange the syndicated finance. By the time Wall Street officially closed at 1600 hours, the US industrial economy had lost nearly one-twentieth of its market value. Had the 'circuit-breaker', a mechanism to suspend institutional transactions automatically undertaken by computer when movement in share prices outside a specified range takes place, not been put into play, the plunge could have been greater.

Interestingly, the failure to obtain the required finance for the consortium was not a consequence of a reluctance on the part of US or European banks. In the past, Japanese banks had provided 30–40 per cent of the funds for leveraged buy-outs (LBOs). Japan's authorities had voiced concern about Japanese banks' involvement in LBOs on several occasions. The UAL deal came at a time when the banks themselves were becoming uneasy about LBOs generally, compounded by a growing concern about trading conditions around the world. So the Japanese banks decided not to participate in the UAL deal. To quote the chairman of the Industrial Bank of Japan, 'We have taken the view that we had a little too much of this kind of debt.'

The New York plunge took place on a Friday afternoon. The London stock market had long since closed for the weekend. More than 48 hours were to elapse before the UK would know how its investors in the country's stocks and shares would react. The UK authorities did their best to have a calming influence. The Bank of England stated that it could see no reason why the London equity market should repeat Wall Street's dramatic fall, since it was not underpinned by leveraged situations. Other authorities worldwide also played down the threat of an international crash in stock market prices. Prices would obviously be marked down, but to what extent to discourage sellers was unknown. One of the first markets to open after Wall Street's fall was Wellington, New Zealand. After an hour's trading, unofficial calculations showed that the New Zealand share market fell almost 240 points, or 10.7 per cent, from its close of 2249.90 on Friday, 13 October. On 16 October, the *Financial Times* reported a general anticipated that the FT–SE 100 Index was likely to start at 50 to 100 points lower (roughly 2 to 5 per cent) when trading began. At 0915 hours on 16 October the following message was flashed by Reuters:

**0915 LONDON FTSE OPENS 157 POINTS DOWN
BUT BUYING SEEN**
THE LONDON FTSE 100 OPENED 157.1 POINTS DOWN, OR SEVEN PCT IN HECTIC TRADE THIS MORNING FOLLOWING FRIDAY'S 190 POINT SLIDE ON WALL STREET BUT DEALERS WERE NOT EXPECTING A RE-RUN OF THE OCTOBER 1987 CRASH AND BARGAIN HUNTING WAS ALREADY EVIDENT.

'Grey Monday', as 16 October 1989 came to be known, was a real 'roller–coaster' on the world's stock markets. London was no exception as the FT–SE 100 (see Table 1.1) revealed during the period. Fortunes were made and lost. At 1249 hours the FT–SE 100 had lost 204.2 points on the previous day's close.

Table 1.1

FT-SE 100 Index

Date	Time	Index	Down on 13.10.89 close	£billion fall in value on 13.10.89 close
13.10.89	1700 hrs	2233.9		
16.10.89	0900 hrs	2076.8	157.1	31.0
	1000 hrs	2101.9	132.0	26.5
	1100 hrs	2091.5	142.4	28.4
	1200 hrs	2057.2	176.7	35.4
	1249 hrs	2029.7	204.2	40.3
	1300 hrs	2038.1	195.8	39.2
	1400 hrs	2053.1	180.8	36.2
	1500 hrs	2078.7	155.2	31.0
	1600 hrs	2113.7	110.8	22.2
	1700 hrs	2163.4	70.5	14.6

From Table 1.1, we can see that after an initial sharp decline, the FT–SE 100 made a significant recovery. London was waiting to see what happened on Wall Street. Needless to say, the Dow Jones recovered its falls of Friday 13 October. At noon in New York (1700 hours in London), the Dow Jones was up 42.83 on its Friday close. By 1700 hours on 17 October (2100 hours in London) it had recovered 88.12 points of its 13 October fall of 190.58 points. The headlines in the *Financial Times* said it all, 'Wall Street rally soothes markets'. The article reported that the continental exchanges were worst hit as the impact of Wall Street's recovery came too late to boost their equity markets. Even an hour's time difference can have quite an effect.

The whole saga of Grey Monday made headlines news in the tabloid press. *Today*, under the headline '£100m Blow as Queen Leads Big-Name Losers', lead with, 'The Queen was first among equals when it came to losing a fortune on Grey Monday. She ended the day £100 million worse off. But it could have been a bigger disaster. At one point, she stood to lose £150 million.' Just to put matters in perspective (not everyone has an equity portfolio of £2.4bn). The case of Alfred Holden, a Merseyside engineer, was cited. He had a holding of UK equities worth £19,054.50 at the close of business on 13 October 1989. By the end of the 'roller–coaster' ride he had lost a 'mere' £727 on the previous day's close, or 3.8 per cent of its worth before the UAL deal went wrong.

Wellcome

The following extracts from the press show how the development of a new product, in this case a drug, had an impact on the share price of a pharmaceuticals company. It had been no secret that Wellcome was working on a cure for AIDS. For some time the share price had reflected the growing hope that a drug would be perfected. The shares were launched on the London stock market in February 1986 at 120p. Their lowest price in 1989 was 400p.

AIDS drug effective says US

AZT, the highly promising AIDS drug developed by Wellcome, the British pharmaceuticals company, is safer and much more effective against the disease than earlier studies had shown, US Government researchers said in a study released yesterday.

The announcement, made in Washington, appears greatly to improve prospects for millions of mostly young people infected with the virus . . . Mr Viren Mehta, partner in drug research company Mehta & Islay, said, 'AZT appears to have fortified its position as the No. 1 drug in AIDS therapy.'

Financial Times, 18 August 1989

(Note: AZT was the code name for the drug later to be known as Retrovir.)

Wellcome drug news lifts hopes and share index

Wellcome, the drug group, dominated the stock market yesterday . . . . American findings which show that Retrovir, the group's anti-AIDS drug, will play an increasingly important role in the battle against the disease, sent Wellcome shares soaring – by 164p to 673p . . . . The progress added more than £1.3bn to Wellcome's stock market value lifting it to £5.6bn.

The drug group's share performance was largely responsible for another impressive advance by the FT–SE share index. It gained 15.5 points with Wellcome's influence accounting for nearly 10 points.

The Independent, 19 August 1989

Rises in share prices are frequently the result of the interaction of more than one factor. The following extracts demonstrate this point. The first extract indicates that a further rise in Wellcome's share price was a consequence of a takeover bid in the pharmaceuticals sector. It is not unusual when a bid is made for a company for the shares of other organisations in the same business to rise. Investors tend to view one takeover as a signal that others are in the air. The second extract reports a rumour that Wellcome itself was going to be the subject of a takeover.

Another shot in the arm

The pharmaceutical sector was galvanised for the second trading day in succession. A $750m bid by Japanese pharmaceutical company Fujisawa for Lyphomed of the US came hard on the heels of Friday's encouraging news on the effectiveness of Wellcome's anti-AIDS drug Retrovir.

Wellcome traded around 15 per cent better ahead of the bid announcement then shot ahead to touch 737p before settling back at 729p, up 56 on the day. 'People are still likely to upgrade even at this level', said one analyst.

Financial Times, 22 August 1989

The Market

Wellcome remained top of the pops in the pharmaceutical sector. The shares . . . climbed afresh to 737p before closing 56p on the day at 729. New demand was fired by a theory that ICI could be interested in making a bid for the company.

Daily Telegraph, 22 August 1989

As with all stock market stories, this situation is ongoing. A week later, the company's share price had slipped back to 693p, 'in market uncertainty over the price being at the right level'.

What happened

At the time of going to press, the company still leads the field with its anti-AIDS drug. As at 1 June 1990, the price of the shares stood at 668p. The 1990 High–Low was 795p–639p.

De La Rue and Norton Opax

This is a story with twists and turns worthy of the plot of a gothic novel. De La Rue is the world's largest printer of cheques, bearer bonds, share certificates, credit cards, vouchers and other pieces of financial paper, and counts an influential number of commercial and central banks (it produces bank notes for 90 countries) among its clients. For five years its profits had risen. On 14 February 1989, the company announced that its profits for the year ending 31 March would fall. Later in February, Norton Opax, the Harrogate-based security printer, approached De La Rue and the companies began talks about possible links. De La

Rue broke off the talks early in June. On 6 June De La Rue announced its profits for the year ending 31 March 1989 – they had fallen from £62.4m to £26.3m. The company's chief executive resigned.

In July 1989, De La Rue announced the sale of its Crosfield Electronics printing technology subsidiary for £235m in cash to Du Pont, the US chemicals conglomerate, and Fuji Photo Film. Crosfield's profits were down from £21.1m in 1987/8 to £5.2m in 1988/9. On the announcement De La Rue's shares rose 3p to 359p. The Lex column in the *Financial Times* commented on the sale of Crosfield and the predicament of its largest shareholder, Mr Robert Maxwell, who had bought 15 per cent of De La Rue after the October 1987 market crash at more than £4 a share. Four days before the announcement of the sale, Scitex Corporation, an Israeli company 27 per cent owned by Mr Maxwell, had bought 6.1 per cent of De La Rue.

De La Rue

The token rise in the De La Rue share price yesterday on the news that Du Pont and Fuji Photo have agreed to buy Crosfield – roughly half of De La Rue – underlines the stock market's dilemma in valuing what is left of the company. De La Rue has got a surprisingly good price for Crosfield, whose erratic profit record and ability to consume cash is the cause of the group's current problems. Yet the planned sale removes the major reason for any bid speculation – the main prop under the current share price.

If it is a done deal, De La Rue shares should go down, not up. But it would be dangerous to count out an unpredictable operator like Mr Robert Maxwell, who is De La Rue's biggest shareholder. He is showing a loss on his investment in De La Rue and the sale of Crosfield to Du Pont/Fuji rather than to Crosfield's main competitor, his own Scitex, presumably removes the main reason for his interest in De La Rue. However, in the absence of mounting a counterbid for either Crosfield or De La Rue, it is difficult to see how he can exit either gracefully or profitably.

Crosfield is being sold at 70 per cent premium to net asset value and an exit multiple of 17 times Crosfield's peak earnings. This is a stiff price but there is just an outside change that Mr Maxwell may be prepared to top the offer and risk the anti-trust problems .

. . . If he does nothing, the bid speculation subsides and so does the value of his De La Rue stake. Putting the company on a normal market multiple suggests De La Rue shares should now be £1 below what they are now.

Financial Times, 19 July 1989

The following day, De La Rue's shares fell 34p. Mr Robert Maxwell did not make a bid for the company, but someone else did a month later. This approach was by a previous character in the De La Rue saga:

Norton Opax launches £484m bid for De La Rue

De La Rue, the group that prints notes for many central banks, yesterday found itself on the receiving end of a £484m takeover bid from Norton Opax . . . . The offer, in the form of cash and Norton Opax shares, was immediately rejected by the board of De La Rue. 'The offer, which is only marginally above the previous closing price, is opportunistic, and fails to reflect the full value of De La Rue', said a statement from Schroders . . . . De La Rue shares closed at 356p, 28p above the level of the offer, as the City anticipated an eventual increase in the Norton terms, or a higher offer from another print company.

The Independent, 22 August 1989

On the same day as *The Independent* announced the takeover bid, its 'View from City Road' column revealed that Mr Maxwell had resisted the sale of Crosfield. While it acknowledged that the bid made commercial sense (as there would be complementary geographical interests), it considered that the bid was too low and advised shareholders to hold out for more. On 1 September, the paper reported a dissatisfaction with Norton's offer.

Pressure on Norton to raise bid

. . . Talks on Wednesday evening with Robert Maxwell, the newspaper publisher who speaks for a 21 per cent holding in De La Rue, were yesterday reported to have been amicable. A source close to Norton said the *Daily Mirror* boss was receptive to the industrial logic of the bid.

However, he is understood to have indicated that he would not be willing to accept the offer at a price of less than 400p per share. On yesterday's share price for Norton of 165p, unchanged, the offer was worth 345p per share, compared with a De La Rue share price of 373p up 3p.

The Independent, 1 September 1989

The story now begins to take an unusual turn. Bowater Industries, the printing and packaging group, were shareholders in Norton Opax. It is believed that Bowater was unhappy that it had not been consulted before Norton Opax mounted its bid for De La Rue.

Norton soars after talks with Bowater

Shares in Norton Opax, the specialist printer which is bidding £484m for banknote group De La Rue, jumped 26p to 191p yesterday after talks with its 26 per cent shareholder, Bowater Industries.

David Lyon, Bowater chief executive, described the meeting as 'informative', but said his company had not made up its mind on the offer. 'They left us some materials which we are studying.'

However, the share reaction lead many market observers to conclude that the talks had not gone well for Norton.

It had sought discussions to win Bowater's support for the bid, but there has been speculation that Bowater might mount its own bid for Norton in view of the dilution of the De La Rue offer would mean for its holding, which would be roughly halved . . . . City analysts were sceptical that Bowater would launch a bid for Norton. Angela Bawtree, of Warburg Securities, said: 'It could be very expensive and would dilute earnings if it were in either cash or paper.'

The Independent, 2 September 1989

The city analysts may have been sceptical, but nothing in this world is a certainty. When Norton Opax mounted its bid for De La Rue, it did not anticipate that the tables would be completely turned.

Bowater in £382m bid for Norton Opax

Bowater . . . has mounted a hostile £382m bid for Norton Opax, attempting to spoil the specialist printer's own £470m offer for De La Rue. 'We believe the De La Rue bid is not in the interests of Norton Opax shareholders', said Bowater chief executive David Lyon. Bowater is itself the largest shareholder in Norton Opax, and yesterday it lifted its 25.6 pc stake to 29.9 pc.

Norton has rejected the offer, and yesterday obtained a court injunction preventing Bowater's adviser Bankers Trust, which formerly advised Norton, from supplying information to co-adviser Morgan Grenfell . . . . The offer is conditional on other Norton Opax shareholders voting down the De La Rue bid at an extraordinary meeting on September 15.

Daily Telegraph, 5 September 1989

The situation was now really 'messy'. On 6 September, Norton Opax increased its bid for De La Rue to £798m. The terms were four Norton Opax shares, 120p of convertible loan stock and 450p cash for each three De La Rue shares. At the prevailing market price (Norton Opax shares had risen by then to 214p), the offer for

De La Rue was 475p for each De La Ruse share – or 410p if Norton Opax shares were valued at 165p, the price of the shares immediately upon the announcement of its bid for De La Rue in August 1989. De La Rue's shares closed just 16p up at 346p. However, the day prior to Norton Opax's extraordinary meeting, it reluctantly abandoned its bid for De La Rue. The Bowater-Norton Opax and De La Rue saga was drawing to a close.

Norton move popular

. . . . Although De La Rue went 17 lower at one point, the shares bounced as dealers considered the possibility of a fourth party making a bid. Likely contenders are said to be the MB Group and Robert Maxwell, who already owns 15 per cent of De La Rue and influences another 6.5 per cent through a 27 per cent holding in Scitex, an Israeli company. De La Rue ended 9 down at 338p, while Norton and Bowater each firmed 2 to 219p and 503p respectively.

Financial Times, 15 September 1989

The final outcome

- *21 September 1989:* Norton Opax's offer for De La Rue lapsed. Acceptances were only received in respect of 137,311 ordinary shares (0.09 per cent). Norton Opax's board recommended shareholders to accept Bowater's offer.

- *29 September 1989:* Bowater had received acceptances in respect of 73,981,716 (52 per cent) ordinary shares in Norton Opax together with acceptances in respect of 29,292,038 convertible preference shares (62 per cent).

- *2 October 1989:* Bowater's offer for the share capital of Norton Opax became unconditional.

- *22 November 1989:* Bowater sold its holding (held by Norton Opax) in De La Rue at a price of 317p per share.

As at 1 June 1990, the price of De La Rue's shares stood at 250p. The 1990 High-Low was 313p–207p. Bowater's shares were priced at 524p. The 1990 High-Low was 524p–434p.

Jaguar

It is unusual for City news to be emblazoned on the front pages of the popular press. However, this story caught the imagination of the tabloids and it was treated to the full works.

Jaguar was privatised by being launched on the market in August 1984 at 165p. The Government retained a 'golden share' which limited bidders to a 14.9 per cent stake. The share was to lapse on 1 January 1991. At the time of the stock market launch it was stressed that with Jaguar's exports to the US, profits were sensitive to the dollar-sterling exchange rate. The press commented on the fact that Jaguar was effectively a one product company, but the flotation was a great success. On 1 September 1989, the share price was 415p. The year's High-Low was 424p–264p. The company's interim results were announced on 13 September and were considerably below expectation. Jaguar declared a pre-tax profit of £1.4m and an operating loss of £2.8m, far short of the City forecasts of about £8m and way down on the 1988 interim pre-tax profit of £22.5m. The comment in the *Financial Times'* Lex column examined the situation.

Jaguar

The trouble with luxury items is that they are, well, a luxury. People can live without them in bad times and even in good times their tastes can be swayed by other, even brighter and glossier products on the market. For Jaguar, a luxury car manufacturing company in a business characterised by high costs and long product development periods, the risks are doubled in spades. Even the fact that Jaguar sales have held up better than most in the US market is a mixed blessing; its rivals will surely attempt to regain market share and the long-term emergence of the Japanese as a competitor is hardly encouraging for price levels. All this investors could bear with equanimity were it not for the currency risk which makes buying Jaguar shares a proxy for investing in dollar call options. Every cent movement in the dollar/sterling rate makes a difference of £3m to Jaguar's pre-tax profits, or, as seems likely for 1989, losses.

Of course, Sir John Egan may well be saving up a few million pounds of profits for 1990, when the golden share runs out and the currency cycle has at last turned in the group's favour. Having hedged at $1.60/£ (compared with $1.70 in 1989), next year's pre-tax profits should be boosted by at least £30m. The markets, which put 5 per cent on Jaguar's share price yesterday, believe they have an each-way bet on the basis that the worse the company performs, the more a takeover becomes likely . . . . Investing in Jaguar shares at much above current levels may be the biggest luxury of all.

Financial Times, 14 September 1989

Nevertheless, Jaguar's shares moved upwards despite the disappointing interim results. The *Financial Times'* market report explained why.

Jaguar hopes
Jaguar fulfilled marketmakers' predictions by rising on news of profits far below even the most pessimistic of forecasts. The logic is that poor figures make the company more likely to be subject to a takeover bid when the Government-held golden share expires at the end of next year.

Mr Stephen Reitman, analyst at UBS Phillips & Drew said: 'The profits this year were of academic interest except in that they underline the problems of currency. Even then they increase the prospects of a takeover attempt.' Dealers suggest Ford of the US as one possible suitor. Jaguar shares climbed 20 to 417p on turnover of 2.3m.

Financial Times, 14 September 1989

On 17 September 1989, the *Sunday Times* ran a piece entitled, **'Jaguar looks to GM for partner'.** Andrew Lorenz, the Industrial Editor, revealed that the company had accepted 'that it needs support from a bigger car group if it is to develop successfully in the long term. The company's favoured partner is thought to be General Motors, the American giant. Jaguar wanted a "big brother" to provide it with engineering resources. Research and development in the luxury car manufacturing industry are very expensive. Sir John Egan recognised that a supportive company may want a share in Jaguar. However, Sir John and his colleagues were "determined to keep Jaguar independent and will insist that any shareholding is a minority stake".' The article stated that Jaguar did not want a link with Ford and was equally cool about BMW.

On 19 September 1989, Ford launched a pre-emptive bid for a minority stake in Jaguar. It took the company completely by surprise. Jaguar's shares closed 62p up at a high for the year of 467p. Sir John was only informed of Ford's intentions late in the afternoon. He emphasised again: 'Our desire has always been to maintain the independence of the company.' The popular press featured the news with banner headlines on their front pages the following day. The *Daily Express* ran with '**FORD BATTLE FOR JAGUAR – Giants Race to Grab Luxury Car Firm**' while the *Daily Mail* chose the clever play on words, '**JAGUAR GETS A FORD ESCORT**'.

The Jaguar camp was far from pleased that Ford had made its move without consultation. 'It is unwelcome and an unwelcome surprise', stated David Boole, Jaguar's Director of Communications. Further displeasure was no doubt caused by Whitehall sources revealing that the Government might not use its 'golden share' to veto a foreign takeover bid. Did this answer the question as to why Ford has pounced for 'the cat', as Jaguar is affectionately known, when it apparently, because of the 'golden share', could not make a quick kill? By now Jaguar's shares were in the fast lane. At one time during the week ending Friday 22 September 1989, the shares had hit 614p. The closing prices for Wednesday–Friday were as follows:

Wednesday 20 September – 510p
Thursday 21 September – 548p
Friday 22 September   – 581p

The *Financial Times'* Lex column on 23/24 September 1989 began, 'Jaguar's share price bahaviour this week looks a classic rebuttal of the efficient market hypothesis . . .'. The final paragraph is extremely relevant to this chapter.

This does not mean that the market is wrong to push the shares to these levels. If an open auction develops, the price cannot rationally be predicted. Jaguar's previous value as an independent is irrelevant, a volume car maker would not only run the company differently, but might find it worth paying extra to deny it to a rival. It would help, though, if a rival actually declared itself.

Financial Times, 23/24 September 1989

The final outcome

- *9 October 1989:* Jaguar and General Motors Corporation announced they were in discussions concerning the possibility of entering into joint venture arrangements.

- *17 October 1989:* Ford of Europe Inc (Ford) announces it has a 10.4 per cent stake in Jaguar.

- *25 October 1989:* Ford announces that when the Government's 'golden share' is relinquished (ie on 1 January 1991), it would be prepared to launch a full bid for the company.

- *31 October 1989:* Jaguar's shares were suspended at 1335 hours pending a statement by the Trade Secretary. In due course, it was announced that the Government would relinquish its 'golden share', provided 75 per cent of shareholders backed any proposals. Trading in the company's shares recommenced at 1622 hours when Jaguar's share listing was restored.

- *2 November 1989:* Ford and Jaguar announced that they had reached agreement on the terms of cash offer for Ford to acquire the share capital it did not already own at 850p per share. General Motors announced that it would not bid for Jaguar.

- *1 December 1989:* Shareholders approved the lifting of the Government's 'golden share'.

- *11 December 1989:* 77.4 per cent of shareholders had accepted the offer which was declared unconditional.

(Also see Chapter 3.)

Polly Peck International

Polly Peck is an international trading company, which for some years has been the world's third largest fruit company. It is also involved with textiles and electronics businesses in exotic locations. This story illustrates that the market's rumours may not always be right. Consequently, prices can dramatically move in the opposite direction when a company announces its intentions. For example, The *Daily Telegraph* reported as follows.

> Polly Peck International, the overseas trader, dropped 14½ to 299p ahead of today's interim report. Gossip around the market suggested that the company could be about to announce a major capital raising operation to fund a significant acquisition . . . .
> One story was that Asil Nadir [the company's Chairman and Chief Executive] could be interested in purchasing Alan Bond's stake in Lonrho, worth about £295m . . . .
> Meanwhile, analysts at Barclays de Zoete Wedd reckon that Polly Peck's interim figures will be very good. They envisage an increase of about 25 pc to £63m and look for about-turn of about £145m for the full year, a prospective multiple of 6.8.
>
> *Daily Telegraph*, 7 September 1989

The following day the press reported Polly Peck's profits up 34 per cent to £64.4m. The company announced there was to be a rights issue. Shareholders could buy three new shares for every seven shares held at a price of 245p. The exercise was to raise

£283m – a modest sum which was a relief to the market. However, it was the reason for the new injection of capital which excited the market – Polly Peck was buying Del Monte's fresh fruit business for US$875m (£647m). Del Monte is the world's biggest distributor of fresh pineapples and the third biggest shipper of bananas. The *Daily Telegraph's* 'City Comment' on the subject ended with the following paragraph.

> Mr Nadir believes Del Monte will provide Polly Peck with both the international spread and status that has long proved elusive. An often sceptical market demonstrated it support with a 70p increase to 369p in the share price on a turnover of 9.7m shares. But, Mr Nadir, who has a habit of giving managers a short shelf life, still has to demonstrate that he has a team capable of managing a million pound business.
>
> *Daily Telegraph,* 8 September 1989

The next day, the *Daily Telegraph's* market report announced.

> The market continued to re-rate Polly Peck after the Del Monte deal and the shares jumped afresh to 422p before closing 44 up on the day at 413p, or 114p above Wednesday's pre-announcement level.
>
> *Daily Telegraph,* 9 September 1989

This also gives another reason for the movement in a company's share price – 're-rating'. In other words, the investor's opinion of a company's prospects changes and is reflected in an upward or downward movement in the share price.

Ferranti International

Ferranti is the second largest company in the UK's defence electronics industry. On 11 September 1989, the company asked the Stock Exchange to suspend the quotation of its shares. The reason for the suspension was that Ferranti was 'reviewing its profits'. They were suspended for an indefinite period at 73½p, against a high for 1989 of 113½p. A statement from the company indicated that it was to face a published loss on overseas contracts managed by ISC Technologies, its US subsidiary. Ferranti would not comment further. The *Financial Times'* market report devoted quite a few column inches to the situation, including the rumours and analysts' views:

The market was immediately awash with various rumours. These included stories about a European group taking a stake in Ferranti, a capital restructuring, or the putting up for sale of various parts of the US interests. However, the favoured suggestion was that the problems involve a missed payment on a significant overseas defence equipment contract that could, according to market specialists, lead to a writedown of some £20m for Ferranti.

Worse still, said analysts, it could lead to intense pressure from institutions for management changes. 'Institutions are now totally disillusioned with the Ferranti board – the game is only just beginning', said one leading watcher of the stock.

Talk in the market suggested that the writedown would be revealed within a week and the annual meeting reconvened in a month. 'The shares will probably be requoted within a week but at nearer 60p than 65p', said an observer.

Financial Times, 12 September 1989

A few City optimists soon began to talk of the shares opening at a figure well above the suspension price when trading recommenced. Their reasoning was based upon the assumption that Ferranti would be 'ripe' for a take over, but this was pure speculation. The market in general was somewhat disturbed at the lack of information in the company's brief statement made at the time of the suspension in dealing in its shares. However, the board of Ferranti was adamant that there would be no further information until a full statement could be made. 'There is no point in going off half cock and half a story', a spokesman for the company commented.

On 15 September, the press reported that the International Stock Exchange was believed to be taking a close interest in the sale of 32 million Ferranti shares by a former deputy chairman of one of the company. The block of shares were sold at 82¼ on 21 July 1989. One of the big stories in the financial pages on 16 September was that Ferranti International Signal had appointed the accountants Coopers & Lybrand to make an urgent review of overseas contracts by its ISC Technologies subsidiary – the first occasion that significant irregularities with contracts had been mentioned.

Clearly, Ferranti could not keep its employees and shareholders in the dark for much longer. According to an exclusive report over the weekend in Milan's daily newspaper *Corriere della Sera,* Italian secret service investigators had identified the Ferranti subsidiary, ISC Technologies, as one of the firms it had linked to the scandal involving credits granted by Italy's Banca Nazionale del Lavoro for military supplies to Iraq.

On Monday 17 September, the chairman of Ferranti International sent letters to the company's employees. What he revealed made headline news.

'Serious fraud' warning by Ferranti chief

The 24,000 employees of the defence electronics company Ferranti were told by their chairman, Sir Derek Alun-Jones, last night that the group may be the victim of serious fraud. Directors fear that Ferranti may have lost £150 million on contracts that did not exist when it took over another company.

Last week Ferranti revealed that it had found 'serious irregularities' at ISC Technologies, a missile company it acquired two years ago when it took over the American-based firm International Signal and control for £400 million.

In his letter to staff Sir Derek said: 'The irregularities are serious and it appears certain that the company and its advisers have been at least misled, and possibly made victim of serious fraud.'

The Serious Fraud Office is being kept informed of the affair and should receive a report at the beginning of next month from the international accountants, Coopers & Lybrand, who have been brought in to review ISC Technologies' accounts.

The Department of Trade is watching the situation closely, as are the Bank of England and the Ministry of Defence.

New capital is being sought for Ferranti in a rescue which may well mean a full takeover. Sir Derek held further meetings at the Ministry of Defence yesterday.

The Ministry had been reported as having opposed the 1987 takeover of International Signal, but agreed with Sir Derek that they had in fact approved the bid in advance of its announcement.

Sir Derek avoids mentioning takeovers in his brief letter to employees.

He states: 'Until the investigation has made further progress, it is impossible to comment in detail.'

'Consequently, press speculation and misinterpretation of the situation is inevitable and we must accept that it is going to be so for a little while yet.'

Daily Telegraph, 19 September 1989

Sir Derek was quite correct regarding press speculation. Reports the following day favoured the German company Daimler-Benz or the UK's British Aerospace as likely contenders for a bid. Naturally, the Government was under pressure to prevent Ferranti falling into foreign hands. By the end of September more detailed information emerged.

> **Ferranti loss in takeover deal was £215m**
> Ferranti is to write off £215 million as a result of its purchase of the American defence company International Signal and Control two years ago, it was announced last night. The dividend promised to shareholders last month will not be paid and it will not be possible to pay future dividends until the firm's capital has been replenished, Sir Derek Alun-Jones, Ferranti's chairman said.
> Ferranti agreed to take over ISC by issuing shares worth more than £400 million, but Sir Derek said: 'it is now clear that the price paid to the shareholders of ISC was substantially inflated as a result of the fraud.'
>
> *Daily Telegraph,* 30 September 1989

In its 'City Comment' column of the same day, the paper commented, 'it would be hard to justify a share price of half the pre-suspension price of 73½p: what will hold up the price is the prospect of a parent bid rather than a crutch. Why should a partner inject capital at a high price relative to the market – never mind last month's market price – to control just 30 pc?'

Events which followed

- *3 October 1989:* Ferranti's share listing was restored. They opened at 45p, peaked at 57p and closed at 55p.

- *10 October 1989:* British Aerospace and Thomson-CSF SA announced that they had decided to co-operate in reviewing all options open to them in relation to Ferranti with a view to making a joint offer. Ferranti's Board made a statement noting British Aerospace's and Thompson-CSF's announcement and stated that indications of interest had also been expressed by a large number of major UK and overseas defence and electronic companies.

- *17 November 1989:* Revised results for the year to 31 March 1989 published.

- *1 December 1989:* Ferranti's Board announced that it was proposing a rights issue of 748,526,432 new Preferred Ordinary shares of 10p at 25p per share on a one-for-one basis.
  British Aerospace announced it was not proceeding to make an offer for Ferranti; Thomson-CSF announced it was continuing to review its options.

- *11 December 1989:* Ferranti sold its Civil Computer Service and Maintenance operations together with the related repair and calibration activities of Ferranti Computer Systems Ltd for £17m cash to Servicetec Ltd.

- *11 January 1990:* Ferranti changed its name to Ferranti International plc.

- *12 January 1990:* Interim results announced for the period ended 30 September 1989. The company reported a net loss of £15m against a profit of £12m in the corresponding period in 1988.

- *18 January 1990:* Thomson-CSF announced that it was currently not pursuing its option to bid for the company.

- *24 January 1990:* Ferranti announced that agreement had been reached with GEC, subject to contract, to sell Ferranti Defence Systems Group (based in Edinburgh) and part of Ferranti's interests in Italy for £310m cash.

- *25 January 1990:* Ferranti announced that agreement had been reached with Finmeccaanica SpA, subject to contract, to sell 50 per cent of Ferranti Italia for £38m cash.

- *5 February 1990:* The Extraordinary Annual General Meeting to be held to approve the disposal of the subsidiary to GEC was adjourned. If the sale was completed by 5 March 1990, the rights issue would be abandoned.

- *8 February 1990:* Ferranti and Thomson-CSF reached agreement to collaborate further in the anti-submarine warfare business. The arrangement was subject to regulatory, Government and shareholders' approval. Thomson-CSF would acquire 50 per cent of a new company comprising the sonar system operation of Ferranti Computer Systems Ltd. The new company would be jointly managed. Thomson-CSF would pay £32m cash.

- *23 February 1990:* Eugene Anderson was appointed chairman and chief executive in succession to Sir Derek Alun-Jones who resigned from the Board. Mr Anderson stated that Ferranti was well on the road to restored financial health.

Other factors affecting share prices

It has been stated that 'anything' can affect the price of a share. A list of factors that could influence the demand and supply, and consequently the price, of a particular stock can never be complete, as not all possible situations could ever be anticipated. However, a good idea of news, events and speculation that can move a share's price upwards or downwards, can be obtained by reading extracts from the market reports. All the following are taken from the *Financial Times'* 'London Stock Exchange Report'.

- The first example illustrates the effect of a broker's recommendation.

> Trafalgar House moved smartly ahead in good volume at the opening in the wake of a bullish note from James Capel. The agency broker upgraded its profits forecast following a positive meeting with Trafalgar's finance director on Thursday. It raised its forecast for next year's profits from £275m to £310m and changed its advice to clients from 'hold' to 'buy'. Capel particularly highlighted the promise in Trafalgar's construction engineering side, as well as the commercial property operation.
>
> The note also suggested that clients should consider switching out of Hanson to buy Trafalgar. Dealers, already unnerved by an overnight purchase of a block of 5m Hanson shares, probably by a New York house, took the opportunity to mark down the price.
>
> While Trafalgar eventually subsided from the day's peak of 407p, to close a net 3 better at 395p, Hanson wallowed, depressed by the overhand, in what one trader described as 'a miserable market'. The shares ended 3½ down at 203p.
>
> *Financial Times*, 9 September 1989

- Rumours abound in the stock market. It may seem strange that the alleged cancellation of hotel rooms could depress a company's share price. However, this is exactly what happened in this example.

> Trading in SmithKline Beecham was also stimulated by rumours that later turned out to have little foundation. The company was said to have cancelled hotel rooms it had reserved in anticipation of launching its potential big selling heart drug Eminase. Fears that the drug had been delayed were assuaged by analysts who said that only the earliest possible approval date would be missed and that the drug should be passed by the end of the year, or by Easter at the latest. SKBeecham ended at 606p down 7 on the day.
>
> *Financial Times*, 9 September 1989

- Analysts can, of course, change their views on a particular share over a short period of time, as is illustrated in this extract:

Cooksons' shares, already groggy from disappointing figures on Thursday, continued to slide. Analysts at County Nat-West Woodmac changed their recommendation on Cookson early in the day from buy to a hold. By the time the trading ended, with the shares 11 down at 349p, they were already saying that investors should be prepared to buy again on further weakness.

Financial Times, 9 September 1989

- Analysts are only human; they do not have a crystal ball which reveals the future. The advice to their clients can only be based on known facts.

Ferranti were extremely active, 9.4m shares changing hands with the share price closing a fraction off at 73½p; analysts are putting the company forward as a second force to GEC in the defence electronics market.

Financial Times, 9 September 1989

As has already been outlined, Ferranti's shares were suspended three days later. By the end of the month it was announced that the company had to write off £215m as a consequence of fraud and that dividends could not be paid until its capital had been replenished. The shares were re-listed on 3 October.

- Periodically, companies organise presentations for investors, ie analysts, institutional investors such as insurance companies and fund managers who are responsible for investing on behalf of pension funds and unit trusts. At such presentations the company outlines its prospects for the future (eg a full order book), as well as indicating its current trading position. If these events are favourable, the company's share price can rise:

Fairline Boats raced 35 better to 635p in the wake of recent presentations to investors.

Financial Times, 9 September 1989

- The prospect of shares reaching a wider audience, for example making them available in the US, can enhance a share's price.

Features in the electronics area included Cable & Wireless which raced up 13 more to 611p in front of the series of US roadshows designed to boost interest ahead of ADS (American Depository Shares) listing.

Financial Times, 9 September 1989

● Press comment can also affect the price of an individual share.

> Grand Metropolitan took a knock in the wake adverse comment in the weekend press and from some City analysts, the shares dropping 15 to 619p on turnover of 2.5m [shares]. The message from both quarters was roughly the same; Grand Met has been concentrating too much on deal making and not enough on its fundamental business. This criticism comes a week after the group announced it was selling the William Hill and Mecca betting shops to Brent Walker for £685m, this just nine months after William Hill was bought from Sears for £331m.
>
> Hoare Govett is one broking house which has publicly expressed concern about Grand Met's voracious appetite for deal-making.
>
> 'We are not arguing that management should pass up a major chance to enhance shareholder value by way of opportunistic disposal' says Hoare on reference to the betting shops sale, 'rather than the cost of doing so confuses the investor and prolongs the period of uncertainty about the effectiveness of group strategy.'
>
> *Financial Times*, 12 September 1989

● Naturally the share price reacts to any company announcement regarding its profitability. However, it is not always the case that an increase in profits leads to a rise in the share price. The reason for what initially looks an odd reaction may be that the market may have been expecting even more.

In response to what is seen as an under-performance, the price falls as disappointed investors sell. Conversely, a good rise in profits could see the shares remaining steady. In such a situation, profits may be expected. In the weeks leading up to the announce-ment, the share price may have edged upwards in anticipation of the results. If the company's announcement causes neither disappointment nor a pleasant surprise the market will view the current price as 'right' and the share price will hold steady.

An announced fall in profits does not always mean that the shares will fall in price. If investors anticipated bad results this will have already been taken account of in the current price of the shares. Consequently, if the fall was not as bad as anticipated, the shares could move upwards. While an unexpected fall in profits generally depresses the share price, the view could be taken that the company is 'right for a takeover'. Here are some examples of how profitability affected the performance of specific shares.

News of the 27 per cent fall in the half-year profits failed to unsettle Coats Viyella, which closed 2½ higher at 172p. Turnover was busy in the stock, with 5.8m shares changing hands in what dealers said was lively two-way business.

Financial Times, 22 September 1989

Laura Ashley weakened 3 to 83p on news of a 36 per cent interim profits fall to £6.5m. Turnover was strong, estimated at 2m shares by one dealer. Analysts trimmed their profit forecasts for the full year with County Nat-West WoodMac, for example, predicting £16m instead of £20.6m.

Financial Times, 28 September 1989

● The resignation of a director can also have an adverse affect on the share price. For example, on 25 August 1989, Mr Jeremy Marshall resigned as chief executive of BAA, the former British Airports Authority. The announcement was made late on Friday afternoon and no explanation was given for Mr Marshall's departure. The market reacted to the resignation on the next trading day by falling 6 to 360p. One dealer summed up the market's view with the words, 'There's no smoke without fire'.

● Bad news from one company can have a spin-off effect on others:

The news that Braniff Airline, the US carrier, is filing for bankruptcy under Chapter 11 of the US Bankruptcy Code for protection from its creditors, hurt shares in British Aerospace and in Rolls-Royce, two companies involved in the production of the Airbus, for which Braniff has placed orders. BAe closed at 631p, down 7 on the day, while Rolls-Royce fell to 182½p, down 3.

Financial Times, 29 September 1989

Market reports in the press may be viewed as a diary which records the ups and downs of the market. Earlier it was stated that 'anything' can influence a share's price. The above extracts give a good cross-section of the influencing factors. By reading the market reports, a greater understanding of what determines share prices can be ascertained. Following the fate of a particular share can be very interesting. The reports can be viewed as a real life 'soap opera' with many thrills and spills.

2

The Reporting of Prices

'A man who knows the price of everything and the value of nothing'
Oscar Wilde's definition of a cynic

The financial pages which are referred to most often are probably those containing share prices. The *Financial Times'* London Share Service is the most comprehensive and daunting of the share price pages, while the *Daily Star* and the *Sun* have the most simplistic listings. The 'quality' press fills the gap in between the two extremes.

The share prices pages

A host of information can appear in share prices pages, as well as prices. In general, the data and number of share prices quoted decrease with the quality of the publication.

Prices

Regardless of the newspaper in which share prices are quoted, it must be realised that the information is printed as at a particular moment in time. In the case of national and regional morning dailies, this will be as at the close of business (1630 hours) on the previous business day. With evening papers the prices quoted can be those at different times of the day. For example, London's *Evening Standard* has three editions each weekday, called 'City Prices', 'Late Price Extra' and 'West End Final' – the actual edition is signified by a red block featuring white lettering in the top right-hand corner of the front page. The prices quoted on the share page are those current at about the time of going to press, in other words at around 0900 hours, 1200 hours and 1330 hours. Commuters speeding their way towards home will therefore be looking at the share-prices current a few hours earlier. The time gap is totally reasonable, but it is easy to forget that the prices are historic when glancing through the columns.

Shares are dealt with throughout a trading session and prices can alter during the day. Of course, some shares are static while others could move progressively upwards or downwards: certain ones may fluctuate within a narrow margin, whereas others may be quite volatile within a wider band. The market is therefore a constantly changing scene. An example may illustrate the point. Shares of BAT Industries closed on 25 September 1989 at 816p. The events of the following day appeared in the *Financial Times'* market report:

> US selling of BAT Industries towards the close of the London market came before the news that the Hoylake Consortium – the current bidder – intends to vote for the board's plans to demerge major areas of its non-tobacco and financial services operations.
>
> Earlier, London had responded enthusiastically to the BAT announcement, driving shares in the beleagured group up by nearly 50p to 864p several pence above the notional share value of Hoylake's £3.5bn offer for the equity. But late deals saw BAT shares fall back to 818p, a net gain of only 2p as the market reacted to Hoylake's surprise announcement.
>
> *Financial Times,* 27 September 1989

However, it is not because the data is historical or because share prices are generally always on the move that investors are unlikely to buy or sell shares at the prices quoted in the press. Quotations for all securities dealt with on the Stock Exchange comprise two prices – *bid* and *offer*. The bid price is the sum at which the investor sells; the offer price is the figure at which he will buy. Only *The Times* quotes both prices – all the other papers quote the middle price, or a figure between the bid and the offer price. This can be illustrated by reference to the *Financial Times* and *The Times* on the same day:

Table 2.1 *Examples of prices quoted*

	The Times		Financial Times
	Bid	**Offer**	**(Middle price)**
	p	*p*	*p*
Boots	282	284	283
Lex Service	356	360	358
Rank Organisation	932	939	936
Trafalgar House	384	386	385

As will be seen from the *Financial Times'* quote for Rank Organisation, the middle price is not necessarily accurate to the last halfpenny. Furthermore, the percentage differential between the two prices is by no means uniform. An extract of bid and offer prices from one day's issue of *The Times* illustrates the point:

Table 2.2   *Examples of Middle (Spread) price quotes*

	Bid p	**Offer** p	**Spread** p	**% Spread of bid price**
Banks (Sidney C)	167	177	10	5.99
Kleen-E-Zee	165	190	25	15.15
Scot Met	164	166	2	1.22
Barclays	514	517	3	0.58
Cable & Wireless	559	564	5	0.89
Nu-Swift	510	530	20	3.92

The reason for the large differences reflects the extent of the market for the stock. Where the volume of trading is high, the spread between the bid and offer price will be lower compared to a stock that is not frequently bought and sold. Similarly, the spread for a 'blue–chip' company will be lower than for one which is not as highly regarded. The situation is not unlike that in the retail trade. Items sold in high volume attract a lower profit mark-up than those where the turnover is lower.

Sectors

There are about 3000 shares quoted daily on the London Stock Exchange. If these were listed alphabetically, the list would be somewhat unwieldy, so the newspapers divide the shares into different sectors. This division does not follow a standard format. Different newspapers have different approaches. For example, the *Daily Telegraph* and the *Guardian* list shares on the unlisted securities market (USM) separately, while the *Financial Times* and *The Independent* incorporate USM shares in the main body of prices, but indicate that the shares are quoted on the USM. Even the names of the sectors vary from one publication to another. For example:

- *Daily Telegraph*   Breweries;
- *Financial Times*   Beers, wines and spirits;
- *Guardian*   Breweries and distillers;
- *The Independent*   Drinks;
- *The Times*   Breweries.

These differences are not major and should not cause confusion. Incidentally, the two newspapers which merely call the sector 'Breweries' do include distillers under this heading. *The Independent* with its more embracing 'Drinks' sector, includes the soft drink manufacturer Nichols (VIMTO), whereas the *Financial Times* includes this company's shares in its 'Food, groceries, etc' sector.

Apart from differences in the names of sectors, certain newspapers have incorporated new names into their page of share prices. For example, *The Independent*, the newest of the nationals, was able to design its page to reflect recent developments such as privatisation issues. Consequently, it listed British Telecom (BT) under its unique 'Utilities' sector, whereas all the other quality nationals listed the company under 'Electricals'. However, *The Independent* too now lists BT under 'Electricals'. Certain companies are also treated differently by the various newspapers, for example, Eurotunnel. Clearly when all is complete it should be categorised under 'Transport' – after all, it will ultimately be in the business of transporting people between the UK and the continent. However, at the moment it is primarily concerned with constructing the link under the English Channel. So, which sector does the company slot into now – 'Building' or 'Engineering'? All the newspapers agree that it is neither of these. *The Times* has no 'Transport' sector, so places it in 'Industrials'. The *Guardian* has a 'Transport' category, but nevertheless includes it in its 'Industrials' sector. The remaining quality press include it under 'Transport'.

There are also other oddities. Boots, the chemists, also makes its own products and develops drugs. Saville Gordon Group, which in the past was primarily scrap metal merchants, has diversified in recent years. Although still involved in the scrap metal business, it is now an insignificant part of the Group's activities. Although involved in engineering, most of the Group's profits emanate from its property investment and development division. Below, the sectors in which the newspapers place the companies are given:

	Boots	*Saville Gordon*
● *Daily Telegraph*	Industrials	Industrials
● *Financial Times*	Industrials	Engineering
● *Guardian*	Stores	Industrials
● *The Independent*	Retailers	Engineering
● *The Times*	Industrials	Industrials

The national press's approach to categorising shares into sectors is far from uniform. When reading different papers, you may have to look around to find particular share prices. However, in time, you will soon learn where to find the company share prices that you require. But do bear in mind that newspapers can juggle shares between sectors occasionally.

Placing a company's share price within a specific sector not only helps the reader to find it quickly, but it also allows the reader to compare the company's share performance with other companies in the same general line of business. The *Financial Times'* London Share Service extends to over two pages, whereas the other quality national press restrict their listing of share prices to one page. It will therefore be appreciated that not every share can be listed in the press. Whereas the *Financial Times* lists most, it does not include everything – for example, Fortnum & Masons is not listed. However, the majority of the most traded shares are listed in the national qualities. The regional and tabloid papers only list a selection.

New issues

New issues, ie shares which have only recently been admitted to the stock market, are listed separately in the *Daily Telegraph, Financial Times, The Independent* and *The Times* under 'Recent Issues'. This situation continues until such time as the prices can be included in the main listing of share prices. The *Daily Telegraph* and *The Independent* include 'Recent issues' in their main price page, while the other two quality newspapers list the new arrivals elsewhere. An exception to placing new issues in a miscellaneous sector of their own was during the 1989 privatisation of the water companies. As so many companies were involved most newspapers immediately placed them into a new 'Water' sector.

Other information

It is not only the prices of shares that are found in the price pages. As has already been mentioned, the newspapers' approach to presenting share prices is not uniform. This is also the case with the additional information presented with the share prices. The *Financial Times'* London Share Service is the most comprehensive. We will now examine the other material in its share price page from Tuesday to Saturday, inclusive. The data published on a Monday differs slightly – this will be examined later.

Tuesday to Saturday
Reading across from left to right, the columns reveal the following.

High-Low. This is most useful data. For example, it could reveal whether the price of a particular share is 'holding steady', if it has been volatile, is at its peak, or has fallen into the doldrums. It will be appreciated that the information merely reflects the situation at two moments in time – ie the year's low and the high. A little more research will have to be undertaken before firm conclusions can be drawn. However, it is a useful guide to see if a particular share is a rising star or one that is in disgrace.

Occasionally there is a small asterisk against the High-Low figures. This indicates that the information has been adjusted to take account of a rights or scrip issue. (Both these terms are explained in Chapter 6 and later in this chapter.)

If the paper changed its High-Low figures at the beginning of each year, the information would not be very useful. Consequently, the data is altered around April. Therefore, in March 1990 the information would cover the period January 1989–March 1990. In May 1990, it would cover the period January 1990–May 1990. The heading of the High-Low column indicates the period which the statistics cover. In the first situation it would be headed 1989/90 and 1990 in the latter.

Stock. This column gives the name of the company, in abbreviated form. For example, J Saville Gordon Group plc appears as Saville Gordon; Midland Bank plc as Midland; British Telecommunications plc, as British Telecom, etc. A value may also appear after some of the companies' names, for example, 5p, 10p or £1. This indicates the shares' nominal or 'face' value. Where no figure is given, the nominal value may be assumed to be 25p. Nominal values have only legal and accounting significance. They do not reflect the market value and they are also no indication of the price at which the shares were originally issued.

While most of the equities quoted on the London market are ordinary shares, ie the shareholders are entitled to a company's earnings and assets after all its prior liabilities, such as loans and trade creditors, have been met (this is why ordinary shares are referred to as 'equities', as the ordinary shareholders are entitled to what remains after prior claims have been met), other classes of shares also exist. These are listed below.

- *'A' or 'Non-Voting' Shares*. These are ordinary shares with no voting rights. The Savoy Hotels' quoted shares are all 'A' shares. Liberty's, the Regent Street store, has voting and non-voting shares.
- *Preference Shares*. Holders of such shares are entitled to a fixed rate of dividend out of profits in priority to anything paid to ordinary shareholders. Additionally, they rank before cumulative preference shares in a repayment of capital in the event of a winding-up of the company.
- *Cumulative Preference Shares*. As preference shares, but in the event of profits being insufficient to pay the fixed rate of dividend to preference shareholders, the deficit will be carried forward and paid when funds are available.
- *Redeemable Preference Shares*. The shareholder has the option to convert such shares into ordinary shares at a fixed time or over a specified period. The rate of conversion may be fixed, or at an increasing ratio of preference to ordinary shares over time.
- *Warrants*. These are not strictly shares, but they give their holders the right to subscribe for ordinary shares or other stock upon payment of a specific sum on a particular day or over a period of time in the future. Eurotunnel shares were issued with warrants.

All the above are quoted immediately below the publication of a company's ordinary share price, where it is applicable.

There are also various symbols used in the stock column. Some are found immediately before the name of the share and others at the end of the column. There is an explanatory key as to what the symbols mean, but it is worthwhile mentioning the most commonly encountered here. Other newspapers adopt a similar approach.

- *A Heart* indicates that the stock is not officially listed on the UK Stock Exchange, but dealings are permitted under the Stock Exchange Rules.
- *A Maltese Cross* indicates that the stock is not listed but is quoted on the Unlisted Securities Market (USM), which was established by the Stock Exchange in 1980 and is a means by which companies that cannot fulfil all the requirements of a full quotation can still market their shares. USM companies are not subject to the same degree of regulation as those with a full listing.

● *The Greek letter Alpha* indicates that the stock is one of the most actively traded issues. The marketmakers are continually buying and selling *alpha* stock and consequently there are firm two-way prices during official trading hours (8.30am to 4.30pm) quoted on the screens throughout the day. Deals are published within five minutes on the marketmakers' screens.

● *The Greek letter Beta* indicates that the stock is not traded as actively as its alpha counterpart. Nevertheless, firm buying and selling prices of *beta* stocks are quoted continuously on the marketmarkers' screens. However, the trades are not published within five minutes as with *alpha* stocks.

● *The Greek letter Gamma* indicates that the stock is traded less actively. Although the marketmakers are able to give continuous two-way quotes on the screens for *gamma* stocks, the prices may only be indicative for minimum deals, though firm for large ones.

(Note: The role of marketmakers, how they deal and the workings of the Stock Exchange Automated Quotations (SEAQ) is fully explained on page 51.)

Price. It has already been explained that the price is the 'middle' price at 1630 hours on the previous working day. Unless otherwise stated, the price is expressed in pence.

The most common of the *Financial Times'* symbols to be found in the price column of its 'London Share Services' are explained below.

● **xd** (ex dividend) indicates that the shares are sold without entitlement to the recently declared dividend. During a period after a dividend is announced up until it is paid, those who sell all or part of their holdings *after* the shares go 'ex dividend' will be entitled to the dividend on the shares they sold. The purchasers of the shares will therefore acquire them *ex div*. Generally the price of the shares will rise as the ex dividend date approaches, then fall by the amount of the dividend on that date. The cut-off point is required for the smooth administration of dividend payments.

Investors who sell *before* the shares go ex dividend are not entitled to the dividend on the shares they sold. Should the company's share register not have been updated in time and consequently a former investor receives a dividend payment for the shares sold, this must be forwarded to the broker concerned with the sale. Seek advice if only part of a holding is sold. Shares generally go ex dividend three weeks before the dividend payment is made.

● **xr** (ex rights) indicates that the shares are sold without entitlement to the recently announced rights issue. A rights issue is the sale of new shares to existing shareholders at an announced ratio, which may be on a one-for-one basis (ie one new share for every share held), a one-for-two, etc. The new shares are generally sold at an advantageous price compared to the prevailing market price.

Investors who sell *before* the shares go ex rights are not entitled to participate in the rights issue. Should the company's share register not have been updated in time and consequently an allotment letter is received for the shares sold, this must be forwarded to the broker concerned with the sale. Seek advice if only part of a holding is sold. Investors who sell *after* shares have gone ex rights are entitled to participate in the rights issue. (Rights issues are explained in Chapter 6.)

●**xc** (ex scrip issue) – the 'c' stands for 'capitalisation' – indicates that the shares are sold without entitlement to the recently announced scrip issue. A scrip issue is the 'free' issue of shares in an announced ratio, which may be on a one-for-one basis (ie one new share for every share currently held), a one-for-two, etc.

Investors who sell *before* the shares go ex scrip are not entitled to the free shares. Should the company's share register not have been updated in time and consequently an allotment letter is received for the shares sold, this must be forwarded to the broker concerned with the sale. Seek advice if only part of a holding is sold. Investors who sell after shares have gone ex scrip are entitled to the scrip issue. (Scrip issues are explained in Chapter 6.)

● *Price at time of suspension* is self-explanatory. Although initial reaction may be that it is a symbol of gloom, this may not be the case. The initiative to suspend dealings in a share may come either from the Stock Exchange or the company. The Stock Exchange has two guidelines for deciding whether or not a company's shares should be suspended: (1) investor protection; and (2) the orderly maintenance of the market.

If a company is about to make a large announcement, the Stock Exchange may decide that a suspension is appropriate. It may not necessarily be bad news; for example, it could be a bid or an agreed merger. On the other hand, it could be the announcement of unexpected losses, as was the case with Ferranti in 1989. A leak of the information could give some investors an unfair advantage.

The Stock Exchange monitors price movements. If particularly large swings are recorded, the authorities may suspect foul play and suspend the company's shares in the interest of maintaining an orderly market. In mid-September 1989, 24 shares were suspended – 12 main market companies; 8 USM companies; and 4 third market companies. Suspension can last up to 3 years. After that period, the shares are usually de-listed.

● **+/−** This column shows the variation in the share price from the price quoted in the previous day's paper. The fall or rise is expressed in the same unit of currency as the middle price in the price column.

Div Net. Shareholders receive UK dividends net of basic rate of tax. This column generally shows the amount paid in pence per share in the company's previous financial year. The 'Div Net' column features a whole host of symbols and letters which are explained in the *Notes* section of the London Share Service page. Some of the symbols in the 'Div Net' column also relate to cover and yield. Other newspapers adopt the same approach, but the *Financial Times* is the most comprehensive. Here is a selection of what some of the symbols and letters signify.

● *Gross*, ie payment is without deduction of tax.

● *Interim since increased or resumed*, ie an interim dividend has been declared for the current financial year. It is either more than, or the same as, the last interim payment.

● *Interim since reduced, passed or deferred*, ie the current interim dividend is either less, has not been and will not be paid, or is postponed until a future date.

C'vr. This column indicates the dividend cover. Not all of a company's distributable profits are paid to shareholders by way of a dividend. A proportion of the profits is retained within the business for expansion. The retained profit will, hopefully, be reflected in the share price as the value of the company increases. The dividend cover is basically calculated as follows:

$$\frac{\text{Net Earnings Per Share}}{\text{Net Dividend}}$$

This is an oversimplification, but will suffice for our purposes. Dividend cover measures dividend safety. Clearly, the higher the level of cover, the lower the risk of a company not maintaining its dividend payment should profits fall in a particular year. A quick scan down this column will reveal that the ratio varies enormously from one company to another. Occasionally, fractional figures will be seen, thus indicating that the dividend payment is being partly met from reserves. Of course, such a situation cannot continue indefinitely.

Y'ld Grs. The gross dividend yield is a general indicator of how the market views a particular share. It may appear strange that dividends are quoted net and the yield is featured gross of tax. The explanation is simple. As mentioned above, shareholders receive dividends net of basic rate tax – indeed, companies generally announce their dividend payment net. However, the market is not concerned with the tax position of individual shareholders. It is the gross yield which is important. The net dividend per share is grossed up as follows:

$$\frac{\text{Net Annual Dividend}}{100 - \text{Basic Tax Rate}} \times 100 = \text{Gross Dividend}$$

The gross dividend yield is calculated as follows:

$$\frac{\text{Gross Annual Dividend}}{\text{Market Price of Share}} \times 100 = \text{Gross Dividend Yield}$$

Gross yields can range from zero to double figures. Theoretically, a low gross yield generally reflects a secure business with the potential of growth – in other words, dividends are likely to increase in the not too distant future and the share price will also rise. On the other hand, a high gross yield indicates that the market considers the company to be a riskier investment.

There could be various reasons for this view. Possibly the industry itself is in decline, or the activities of the business are commercially or politically risky. However, it must be remembered that a company's dividend policy is decided by its board of directors. The amount of dividend it declares is an arbitrary decision. Therefore, the gross dividend yield must not be used in isolation in making an investment decision.

The price earnings (PE) ratio. This is a simple concept. It is basically calculated as follows:

$$\frac{\text{Current Share Price}}{\text{Earnings per Share}^1}$$

(^{1} Over the last 12 months – ie for the last full trading year, or on an interim to interim basis.)

The PE ratio may be regarded as a 'confidence' ratio. The higher the PE figure, the higher the market's regard for the company. A high PE could indicate that the share price is bounding ahead of the company's most recently published earnings.

Glancing down the PE columns, you will notice that there are one or two gaps. For example, the ratio is not given for certain banks, insurance companies and mines and for investment trusts. This is because such factors as taxation, income distribution or objectives makes the ratio either meaningless or irrelevant.

There is one aspect of the PE ratio that the reader of the financial press will find particularly bewildering. This is that the ratio varies from one newspaper to another. For example, here are some PE ratios extracted from the *Daily Telegraph* and the *Financial Times* on the same day.

Table 2.3 *Price/Earnings Ratios as reported 28 October 1989*

Company	Daily Telegraph	Financial Times
AIM Group	17.8	12.8
Bodyshop	57.0	53.3
Foseco	10.1	9.3
Geest	13.8	14.2
Rank	11.0	11.3
Wellcome	40.0	34.8

It is stressed that these figures are extracted to make a point. On many occasions the reported ratios agree or differ purely because of rounding up or down. It is also not only newspapers who differ on the calculation of PEs, brokers also report varying PE ratios. The reason for this is that although the concept of the ratio is simple, one of the factors in the calculation is complex. The current share price is a matter of fact. It is what constitutes 'earnings per share' where differences arise and there are three basic methods of defining earnings: the nil method; the net method; and the maximum method, all of which achieve different results.

There is also another area for differences in PE calculations. The development of UK fiscal law over recent years has resulted in tax provisions being more subjective than in the past. If adjustments are made, for whatever reason, to the figures supplied by a company, variations in PE ratios will arise. It must also be borne in mind that the newspapers' PE ratios are historic. City analysts are naturally more concerned with the future than the past.

Monday

On a Monday (or a Tuesday if there has been a Bank Holiday), the *Financial Times* and the other quality newspapers take the opportunity of varying the information contained in their share price pages. Reading from left to right this is the data that the *Financial Times* includes in its 'London Share Service'.

Market Capitalisation. This is one indication of a company's size. It is derived by multiplying the current share price by the number of shares issued. It is important to note that the figures are calculated for each class of share. Where a company has issued more than one class of share, no figure is given for the total stock market capitalisation of all classes of shares. For example, take Clifford Foods; the *Financial Times* reads:

Market Cap

£m	Stock
12.5	Clifford Foods
46.4	Do 'A' N–V

In other words, the ordinary voting shares in this example are capitalised at £12.5m and the ordinary non-voting shares at £46.4m. The total market capitalisation is therefore: £12.5m + £46.4m = £58.9m.

Stock. The information contained in this column is exactly the same as for normal issues Tuesday to Saturday inclusive.

Price. This is the middle price on the previous business day, ie on a normal Monday, the price will be as at approximately 1630 hours on the previous Friday. On the Tuesday after Easter, the price will be as at the close of business on Maundy Thursday.

Div Net. As explained on page 45.

Y'ld Grs. As explained on page 46.

Last xd. This column gives the date when the shares last went 'ex dividend', ie the date at which a buyer had no right to any previously declared dividend payment.

Dividends Paid. This column contains important information for those who rely on dividends for an income. This gives the month or months that dividend payments are made. Most companies declare and pay a dividend twice a year, whereas some choose to make annual or quarterly payments.

Cityline. This is a *Financial Times'* share price service. By dialling 0836 43 plus the unique four digit number in this column, callers are advised of the latest price of the share in question. Calls are charged at 38p per minute and 25p off-peak, including VAT. The pre-recorded voice also gives the offer-bid price, the market report, including the latest indices.

How do newspapers gather share prices?

Introduction

Before explaining how the prices of shares published in the press are obtained, it is first necessary to examine briefly the basic workings of the Stock Exchange, or, to give it its proper title, the International Stock Exchange of the United Kingdom and the Republic of Ireland Limited. The Stock Exchange is first and foremost a market. It is where Government and industry can raise capital and where investors can buy and sell their securities freely. The Exchange is concerned with such matters as membership, dealing rules and settlement rules (ie being paid for and paying for securities sold or purchased), as well as ensuring that the companies quoted in its market meet certain requirements. The Exchange has always had a communications function. It conveys both company news and market information to practitioners and to the public. Since its foundation in the eighteenth century, the Exchange has policed itself, and has adapted its methods of surveillance and regulation, and its rules and codes of practice to meet the changing environment. Needless to say, these have become increasingly complex as the Stock Exchange itself has developed.

Until 27 October 1986, the Exchange comprised stockjobbers and stockbrokers. The jobbers were wholesalers of stocks and shares. They earned their income by the difference in the prices at which they bought and sold. These had to be competitive if they were to survive and naturally their objective was to trade at prices which equated supply and demand. Jobbers did not deal direct with the public. It was the brokers who undertook the transactions on the floor of the Exchange on behalf of buyers and sellers. This system had built-in consumer protection. In a situation where jobbers were competing with each other for business, transactions would be conducted at price levels determined by market forces. Brokers had no financial interests in the shares that they recommended and therefore their advice was always impartial. Their income was obtained from the commissions they charged clients for undertaking transactions on the Exchange.

This system worked well, but during the 1970s and 1980s, it became apparent that the market (internationally and nationally) was changing. The financial institutions, such as pension funds and insurance companies, were playing an increasingly important role. The size and volume of institutional investment began to place a strain on the jobbers' financial resources. In order to spread their business risk and increase their capital, jobbing firms began to merge. Consequently, this reduced the number of firms competing for the brokers' business. Financial houses were also becoming more multinational as they developed international networks in order to improve the service to their clients.

The catalyst finally came in 1983, when the Stock Exchange reached agreement with the Department of Trade and Industry to abolish the system of minimum commissions. In return, the Office of Fair Trading agreed to drop its case against the Exchange in the Restrictive Practices Court.

Minimum commissions were abolished on 27 October 1986, which became known as the day of 'Big Bang'. As a consequence of changes in its membership rules (namely that member firms could be owned by a single outside corporation), London's Stock Exchange now has the most international membership of any of its counterparts anywhere in the world.

The system of dealing was also altered. Member firms became broker/dealers able to act as both an agency broker and as a principal. In other words they could both buy and sell shares on their own account. Firms of brokers/dealers also have the option of becoming committed marketmakers. In other words, they are required to make markets at all times in their registered stocks. This means that they must be ready to buy such stocks at all times during business hours. Strict rules were introduced requiring firms to stand by their prices at all times. Although many firms still only act as agents for their clients, most of the larger ones have developed in both activities.

The most dramatic visible effect of Big Bang is that trading is no longer undertaken on the floor of the Stock Exchange building at Old Broad Street in the heart of the City of London. The Exchange's UK equity market is now a screen-based, quote-driven market, with no physical market floor. On the day of Big Bang the Stock Exchange Automated Quotations system, SEAQ for short, was introduced. It is a computerised price display which uses terminals in brokers' and investors' offices throughout the UK. It provides all market users with up-to-the-minute access to dealing information.

How SEAQ works

Using the SEAQ system, accessed by terminals located in their own dealing rooms, firms of competing marketmakers input prices in the securities in which they are registered, quoting firm buying and selling prices in a range of sizes from 1000 shares upwards (5000 for the most actively traded alpha securities). The average largest screen size in alpha securities is 85,000 shares.

SEAQ is operated by the Exchange's international equity market department. Its staff receive the price quotations from each individual marketmaker, and validate the information to ensure that no excessive price jumps are accepted unless confirmed by the marketmaker. The individual quotations in each equity are then arranged together on the SEAQ page, which is then displayed on the Exchange's viewdata system TOPIC and broadcast all over the UK. A broker wishing to transact business for his client can then simply select the relevant screen page on TOPIC and view all the competing price quotations in a chosen stock. For the top 800 UK equities, SEAQ selects the best bid and best offer prices, which are then displayed prominently on a 'yellow strip'. This allows the broker to see immediately the most advantageous price.

For the most active shares there is a constantly updated display of the volume of shares traded and details of bargain prices are published immediately for approximately 75 per cent of all transactions. Although most investors employ a broker to transact their business for them, marketmakers are able to deal directly with investors, and frequently do so, particularly with the large institutional investors.

Share prices published in the press

As has already been explained, the share price published in the press, with the exception of *The Times* which publishes both the bid and offer price, is the middle price (ie halfway between the bid and offer quote). The morning newspapers quote the prices as at the close of business on the previous business days. Papers which have one or more editions during the day, for example London's *Evening Standard* and provincial evening newspapers, quote the middle price at the time of going to press. For most evening papers, this is early in the afternoon.

The *Financial Times'* reporters obtain prices direct from the Stock Exchange, and extract the information from the SEAQ system. Other newspapers obtain their share price data from specialist companies. For example, London's *Evening Standard* uses the services of Extel as does the *Guardian*, *The Independent* and *The Times*. The *Daily Telegraph* obtains its prices direct from the Stock Exchange.

Share price indices

Introduction

There are various financial indices which act as barometers of the stock market's progress. News bulletins on the radio frequently refer to rises or falls in the FT-SE 100 Index or *Footsie*. Indeed, some radio stations routinely quote its latest position every hour. The financial pages always quote various indices. In times of financial crisis, Footsie can make headline news on all news media from television to local radio, the tabloid press to the national 'qualities'. Falls in an index are translated into billions wiped off the values of shares. The figures are so large that most people cannot comprehend the sums involved. This section explains the difference between the FT Ordinary Share Index, the Footsie and the All-Share Index and gives guidance on the significance of each for the small investor.

FT Ordinary Share Index

The FT Ordinary Share Index (the FT Index) started life in 1935. Its greatest strength is the fact that it is well established and is sensitive to price movements. It started life in the *Financial News*, which was later absorbed into the *Financial Times*. Its original name, the 30-Share Index, clearly indicates that it is not an all-embracing indication of the market's performance, as it reflects the price movements of only 30 shares. Later it was renamed the Industrial Ordinary Share Index as its original objective was to reflect the progress of the shares of British industries. However, over the years, the make-up of the British economy has switched from an industrial bias to embrace retail and service industries as well as manufacturing companies. In 1984, National Westminster Bank was included in the Index and the word 'industrial' was dropped from its title.

However, this was not the first change in the selection of companies that constitute the FT Index. Over the years some have been lost through mergers and liquidations. Other companies have been removed as they were no longer considered to be representative of British industry or commerce. The privatisation of the public utilities in recent years has also necessitated a change in the selection of companies which comprise the Index. Although the 30 companies which currently comprise the Index are diverse in nature, they have one thing in common – all are 'blue-chip' companies which are heavily traded on the Exchange. As such companies are the first to respond to any change in market sentiment, the Index is considered to be a good general indicator of the market's mood.

Technically, the FT Index is unweighted and geometric in form. It is calculated as follows:

$$100 \times \frac{a}{A} \times \frac{b}{B} \times \frac{c}{C}, \text{ and so on for all 30 shares a–z+4 others}$$

where: a = the current share price of share A; and A = the share price at the chosen base date.

When it was first introduced, the Index was only calculated daily. Later it was calculated each hour, while today, thanks to the SEAQ system, it is calculated every minute. All the major newspapers at least quote the FT Index at the close of business on the previous working day, together with its change (plus or minus) on its opening position. The *Financial Times,* being the City's 'bible', not surprisingly goes to greater lengths. For the convenience of its readers, the Index as at the close of business on the previous working day, appears on its front page, in the 'Markets' table and at the head of the 'Lex' column. On the basis that the Index at two particular points in time is not of great value to professionals, more details of the Index are included on the back page of the paper's 'Companies and Markets' section in a table headed '*Financial Times* Stock Indices'. Not only are the previous day's high and low given, but the level of the Index is also recorded at every hour on the hour. Its level a year ago and the year's high and low are also given, together with its all-time high and low. As a matter of interest, its all-time low was 49.4 on 26 June 1940.

One of the reasons why it was decided to base the FT Index on a geometric rather than an arithmetic mean is that with the former it is easier to replace constituents. Had the arithmetic approach been adopted, it would have been necessary to rebase the Index every time one company was replaced with another. Moreover, the geometric method curbs the effect of dramatic price movements. For example, should one share halve and another double, assuming both start from 100, the arithmetic mean would be 125, while the geometric mean would remain at its original level of 100. However, the counter-effect of the geometric method is that it has a bias towards downturns over time, thus when it is decided to replace an ailing or failed company in the Index, the negative bias outweighs any positive movements for some time. Consequently, the FT Ordinary Share Index is not considered a good yardstick in the long term.

FT-Actuaries Share Indices
Because of the defect over time of the FT Ordinary Share Index, the FT-Actuaries series of indices was formulated in 1962. It is essentially a professional's yardstick of the performance of equities. When fund managers claim to have 'beaten the Index', they are referring to the FT-Actuaries All-Share Index which is commonly referred to as the FT All-Share Index. It is in fact the flagship of the FT-Actuaries series. There are around 700 constituents which cover a very broad spread of companies.

The Indices are compiled jointly by the *Financial Times*, the Institute of Actuaries and the Faculty of Actuaries and are based on a formula which relates current market capitalisation to the market capitalisation at a base date, duly adjusted of course to take account of capital changes. Technically, it is a weighted arithmetic average. Because of the number of constituents, the FT All-Share Index is an excellent reflection of the whole market. Indeed, its constituents account for 80 per cent of the UK equity market capitalisation. Because of its method of formulation it behaves in much the same way as an actual portfolio. While the shares of certain companies in the Index will be actively traded, others may change hands less frequently. Consequently, the Index appears to slowly mirror the FT Ordinary Share Index which comprises 30 actively traded companies. Because of its construction, the All-Share Index is a more reliable long-term measure of the market's performance.

The All-Share Index is broken down into 34 sub-sections and 5 groups. For example, as at 17 October 1989, the Consumer Group embraced 184 companies, broken down into the following sub-sections:

No of Companies	Sub-section
23	Brewers and distillers
20	Food manufacturing
14	Food retailing
14	Health and household
34	Leisure
15	Paper and packaging
18	Publishing and printing
32	Stores
14	Textiles
Total = 184	

An index is given for each group and sub-section. It is therefore possible to assess, say, the performance of a particular food retailer's share against the food retailing sub-section. Information is also given relating to earnings, yields and PE ratios for groups and sub-sections. The indices of 23 sub-sections are combined to give the Industrial Group Index. The 500 Share Index comprises the Industrial Group Index together with the oils and gas sub-section. The table of FT-Actuaries Share Indices is expanded on a Saturday to include highs and lows.

Because of the complexities of its compilation, the FT-Share Indices, and thus the FT All-Share Index, are only calculated once a day, shortly after the close of business. (Note: the FT-Actuaries Share Indices are only published in the *Financial Times*.)

FT-SE 100 or 'Footsie'

The *Financial Times* – Stock Exchange (FT-SE) 100 Share Index (Footsie) was established on 3 January 1984, with a base value of 1000. Its 100 constituents are selected from the leading UK companies listed on the Exchange. It was introduced for various reasons. The mathematical bias of the FT Ordinary Share Index has already been mentioned. It also comprises a mere 30 companies and is therefore somewhat narrow and not a true representation of the market generally.

There are additional reasons why a new index was required. With the increasing competition from overseas markets it became essential to have a minute-by-minute index which mirrored price movements of UK equities – the FT All-Share Index is only calculated after the close of business each day. There were also pressing demands from the new London Traded Options Market and Financial Futures Market for a constantly updated index so that products could be developed to allow investors to hedge or take a view on future market trends by way of a single transaction. It was against this background that the Footsie came into being.

The companies which constitute the FT-SE 100 are selected by their market value, ie total shares issued multiplied by the price of the shares in the market. Those selected account for almost 70 per cent of the total market value of the UK equity market. For various reasons, some companies with large market values are excluded from the Footsie for one of the following reasons:

- the company is considered to be resident overseas;
- it is a subsidiary of a company already in the Index;
- no dividend is anticipated to be paid; or
- the company's shares do not change hands.

As with the FT Ordinary Share Index, the original selection of the constituent companies is not fixed for all time. However, changes are kept to a minimum. A company will only normally be removed if it has fallen below 110 in its market value rating and if its replacement has moved into the top 90 vis-à-vis its capitalisation. Naturally, acquisitions and mergers can result in changes. In the event of a company's shares being suspended, matters are usually left in abeyance until the situation is resolved, or the suspension is lifted.

It is important that the constituents are carefully monitored. Indeed, the committee that made the original selection of the 100 companies keep the Index under regular review. Its decision regarding any changes is based upon information supplied by various departments of the Exchange which monitor the Index on a daily basis. The committee ensures that any new constituent company is suitable before agreeing to any change. A reserve list of acceptable companies is kept should a vacancy in the Index arise. The full list of companies in the Index as at 1 January 1990 is shown in Table 2.4.

Table 2.4 *Constituents of the FT-SE Index as at January 1990*

British Petroleum
BAT Industries
Hanson
ICI
GEC
RTZ
Marks & Spencer
Prudential
Bass
Tesco
GUS 'A'
Boots
BOC Group
Cadbury Schweppes
Trusthouse Forte
Fisons
Argyll Group
Pearson
BAA
Rank Organisation
Whitbread 'A'
MEPC
Sears
British Telecom
Glaxo
BTR
Wellcome
Grand Metropolitan
Unilever
National Westminster Bank
Sainsbury's
Lloyds Bank
Enterprise Oil
Ladbroke Group
Land Securities
General Accident
P & O 'Deferred'
Thorn-EMI
Guardian Royal Exchange
BET
Legal & General
AB Foods
Trafalgar House
Tarmac
Rolls-Royce
Carlton Communications
Shell
British Gas
SmithKline Beecham
Barclays

Guiness
Cable & Wireless
Reuters 'B'
Allied Lyons
Racal Electrical
Midland Bank
British Steel
Sun Alliance
Royal Insurance
Reed International
Abbey National
Commercial Union
Rothmans International
TSB Group
Reckitt & Colman
Pilkington
Lonrho
United Biscuits
Polly Peck
British Airways
STC
Ranks, Hovis Macdougall
Hawker Siddeley
RMC Group
Kingfisher
Burmah Group
GKN
Sedgwick Group
Northwest Water
Courtaulds
Redland
Hillsdown Holdings
Hammerson Properties
Ultramar
Smith & Nephew
BICC
Lucas Industries
Globe Investment Trust
Inchcape
Maxwell Communications Corporation
Royal Bank of Scotland
British Aerospace
Scottish & Newcastle
Standard Chartered
ASDA Group
Blue Circle
Burton Group
Thames Water
Cookson Group
LASMO

Technically, the Footsie is a weighted arithmetic index, which means that a change in price is weighted by the issued share capital of the company. Consequently, a 10 per cent movement in the shares of the smallest company in the Index has less 'weight' than a 10 per cent movement in the company with the largest market capitalisation. The prices are taken from SEAQ and the Index is calculated by one of the Exchange's computers each minute of the day from 0830 hours until about 1630 hours. As it is an arithmetic average, the base value has to be re-calculated whenever a constituent company issues more shares. This ensures that only a movement in its share price and not an increase in the number of shares, has a direct effect on the Footsie.

Since 3 May 1984, it has been possible to trade FT-SE contracts on the traded options market. These are based on the same concept as those in individual securities. The main difference between the two is that the Index options are specially designed to enable investors to profit from price movements in the stock market generally, rather than in individual company shares. Investors who have had the experience of being right about movements in the market as a whole, but have chosen to invest in shares that have gone against the trend, will appreciate the significance of index options. Index options now account for about 10 per cent of the daily contract volume of the traded options market.

Other indices

The FT Ordinary Share, the FT-Actuaries Share and the FT-SE 100 are all based on major UK equities. However, the following are other indices that appear in the national press.

- *FT Gold Mines Index.* This index comprises 24 South African mines.

- *USM Index.* Datastream's index of the Unlisted Securities Market.

- *FT-Actuaries World Index.* This was launched in 1987 and was designed primarily for professional investors. It comprises nearly 2400 equities from 24 countries. As well as the individual country indices there are also 11 regional indices, eg Europe, Nordic, Pacific Basin, the World excluding Japan, etc. The flagship of the series is the FT-Actuaries World Index.

- *Local Market Indices.* The world almost knows no financial boundaries. Consequently, the UK papers quote the equivalent of the FT-Ordinary Share Index from countries spread alphabetically from Australia to the United States. The most familiar indices quoted are the Dow Jones and Standard and Poors from the US; Hong Kong's Hang Seng Bank; and Japan's Nikkei.

Other equity share prices

USM

Both the *Financial Times* and *The Independent* list Unlisted Securities Market (USM) shares among the shares of those companies with a full Stock Exchange listing. Therefore, in these two papers, to ascertain the price of price of the shares of an eletrical company quoted on the US for example, one makes reference to the 'Electricals' sector. However, the other quality nationals list USM companies in a separate category of their own. In the case of *The Times*, this is away from the main share price page. When USM shares are contained in a separate category, the shares are listed *en bloc* alphabetically and not alphabetically by sector. As the number of USM companies is small compared to the main market, this approach does not hinder the search for a share price for a particular company.

Recent issues

Recent issues are also generally listed separately from the main list of share prices. The only exception in recent years was the privatisation of the 11 water companies late in 1989. As the group constituted a completely new sector, several papers placed then in a 'Water' or 'Utilities' section immediately. However, new issues are normally listed separately until the main share listing can be rearranged to accommodate the new arrivals. The only exception appears to be the *Guardian*. The *Daily Telegraph*, *Financial Times*, *The Independent* and *The Times* all have a 'Recent Issues' section. The *Daily Telegraph* and *The Independent* incorporate this into its main shares page, while the *Financial Times* and *The Times* include their 'Recent Issues' elsewhere. In the case of the *Financial Times*, this is located under 'London Market Statistics', which is quite a few pages back from its 'London Share Service'. The amount of information divulged varies from one paper to another, but here is an explanation of what may be published.

- *Issue Price*. This is the price at which investors contract to buy the shares. Certain shares are not sold to the general public, but to a specific group of buyers. This is known as a 'placing'. A symbol may signify this.

- *Amount Paid Up*. The letters FP indicate that the issue price was fully paid at the time of issue. However, this is not always the case. Most privatisation issues are purchased in instalments, so holders of the partly paid shares have to pay the next instalment when it falls due.

All the other information such as High-Low (generally since the issue was made) and Closing Price is self-explanatory. The procedure for applying for new issues is outlined in Chapter 6.

Rights issues

A rights issue is an issue of new shares to existing shareholders, usually at a price below the current market price of shares. Rights issues are made by provisional allotment letters and are sent to shareholders on the company's share register at a particular date. Rights issues will be dealt with in greater depth in Chapter 6. Here we will concentrate on the information contained under the 'Rights Issues' sections of the press.

In December 1989, Fisons announced a one-for-eight rights issue at 290p. This means that a shareholder with 800 shares would have the right to buy a further 100 at 290p. Only the *Financial Times* and *The Times* publish the price of rights issues on a regular basis. Figure 2.1 shows the appropriate line in the *Financial Times'* rights offer section of its 'London Market Statistics' on 5 January 1990.

Figure 2.1 *Rights offers*

1989/90

Issue price p	Amount paid up	Latest renun-ciation date	High	Low	Stock	Closing price	+ or –
290	Nil	2/2	62pm	41pm	Fisons	54pm	−1

pm = premium

What does this information tell us? The 'Latest Renunciation Date' means that shareholders have until 2 February either to sell or take up their rights. If they sell, they will receive around 54p for each entitlement to buy a new share – less the broker's commission. Alternatively, should they decide to take up the rights, they will have to pay 290p for each share to the company's registrars by 2 February.

Which paper?

Undoubtedly the *Financial Times*, or the 'Pink Un' as it is colloquially known, is *the* UK's financial newspaper. The catch-phrase 'No FT – No Comment' may sound boastful, but the fact remains that on the occasions in the past when the paper has not appeared for whatever reason, the City has become somewhat 'jittery'. With a wealth of financial information now available from screen-based sources, the impact of the non-appearance of the FT may not be as great as it was in the past, but it would never-theless be greatly missed by the professionals.

The majority of small investors who wish to monitor the progress of the stock market simply will not have the time to wade through the *Financial Times* each day, but its Saturday edition and weekend section might be a good weekly choice. As well as all its regular features and prices, it also contains a personal finance section.

Which daily newspaper you read to monitor the stock market is a matter of personal choice. All the 'qualities' have good financial pages, while the tabloids offer varying degrees of coverage. You must examine what is on offer and decide which best suits your needs. Table 2.5 details the main features found in a selection of daily national newspapers and in Chapters 4 and 5 other sources of financial information are explored.

Table 2.5 *Analysis of share prices quoted*

Paper	No of share prices quoted	High-Low	Div net	Cover	Yield gross	P/E
Financial Times	2946	√	√	√	√	√
Guardian	1295	√	–	–	√	√
Daily Express	527	–	–	–	–	–
Daily Mail	468	–	–	–	–	–
Daily Telegraph	1762	√	–	–	√	√
The Times	1710	√	Gross	–	√	√
Today	773	√	–	–	–	–

3
What the Papers Say

'Bargains made in speed are commonly repented at leisure' George Pettie,
1576

Tips, news and views

Where do newspapers obtain their financial information? Share
prices are supplied either direct from the Stock Exchange, or by an
agency which in turn obtains them from the Exchange. The
reporting of a company's results is another straightforward
matter. The newspaper's journalists attend the company's press
conferences and obtain the facts and figures. Newspapers'
comments on companies' performances are a different matter.
Clearly, a journalist will have his own views. Nevertheless, it is
what the market thinks that is important. A journalist will know
where to go and who to ask to gauge the market's reaction to a
particular set of figures. It will not be restricted to one source only.
By speaking to stockbroking firms whose analysts closely monitor
the company, marketmakers who deal in the shares and other
sources 'close to the company', such as institutions, you will be
able to ascertain the market's reaction to the results.

An experienced reporter responsible for compiling a paper's
market report may have spent years involved with the City. Such
reporters should know what to expect following a particular
announcement. However, more importantly, they will know who
to ask if they hear of something interesting. By developing a
rapport over many years with those 'in the know', they will
instinctively home in on a reliable source. However, they are also
fully aware of the penalties of 'insider-dealing' and contrary to
some popular opinion, they will know when to cease their
questioning and retire gracefully from the scene.

To write a lively market report requires a combination of
technical knowledge and a way with words. Another way to view
the situation is to say that it requires a technical ability combined
with an artistic skill. How dull it would be if a market report

simply stated that a particular share went up while another went down. Some individuals who have never read a market report may consider that such columns are turgid affairs anyway, but rest assured, this is not the case. The reports are not without humour on occasions. For example, here is an abbreviated extract from Norman Whetnall's market report in the *Daily Telegraph* on 7 February 1990.

Rudderless Equities in Voyage Downstream

London marketmakers offered various descriptions of the day's trading, including drab, dismal, lifeless and lack-lustre, but 'rudderless' was probably the most apt until opening weakness on Wall Street saw things going rapidly downstream.

The FT-SE 100 Index, which was just holding above its chart support level of 2335 before New York came in, finished 27.3 down on the day at 2321.1. The FT-30 Index closed 25.4 lower at 1835.6.

Market turnover remained low at 407.8m, but there was some good business in **Sears**, unchanged at 100p after a trading total of 11m. **TSB**, apparently the most active share of the day, was flattered with a reported volume of 15m, but somebody had pressed the wrong button and the actual turnover was more like 5m. . . .

London punters who had taken bull positions in **Euro-Disneyland** ahead of Monday's entry of first-time American buyers were congratulating themselves as further support from the United States sent the price to a new high of £11.88.

Thank you very much, they said, and promptly took profits. In the event, the shares reacted to close 10 down on the day at £11.03.

Gilts managed a modest technical rally – prices had gains of £1¼ but dealers remained extremely cautious ahead of the American auctions where the major test will be tomorrow's 30-year bonds.

Composite insurance issues trended lower as the weather men predicted new storms. **Commercial Union** slipped 7 to 505p. **General Accident** 10 to £11.63 and **Guardian Royal** 10 to 242p. . . .

There was fuel for thought in the oil sector as Warburg and Nomura took different stances on **Ultramar**, finally 11 down at 374p. Warburg analysts were recommending a switch out of Ultramar at 650p, after 653p, while those at Nomura put out a 'buy' circular on Ultramar.

Commenting on the opposition views, one neutral observer said: 'That's what makes a market. . . .

Gold shares kept on the move as selective buyers continued to nibble in a thin and sensitive market. **Harmony** climbed 59 to 810p, while gains of 31 were scored by **Elandsrand**, at 731p.

Loraine, at 309p, and **Western Areas** at 209p. Bullion closed $421¼. . . .

Tailpiece

A Channel Islands reader reckons that the shares of **Campari International**, down from last year's high of 342p, are oversold at the present 188p and he may be right.

The market here was soured by September's cautious interim statement, but it is felt that the likely profit shortfall will not prove too serious – analysts at Barclays de Zoete Wedd are looking for £4.2m, against £4.8m, for a prospective multiple of 5.7.

This sporting leisurewear and camping equipment group has strong finances and 50 pc of sales overseas, hence the view that it is a fair degree of insurance against current home pressures on consumer spending.

Daily Telegraph, 7 February 1990

This report is written in a highly readable style. However, one or two of the terms used warrant further explanation.

- *Market turnover:* the total number of shares traded on the day the report covers.
- *Volume:* another term for market turnover.
- *Punters:* investors who are taking a short-term view. In other words, they are buying shares with a view to taking profits in the near future.
- *Bull positions:* bulls are stockmarket optimists – they expect share prices to rise. 'Taking a bull position' is to buy shares in the expectation of an increase in prices.
- *Technical rally:* can also be called a short-term bounce. It is normally a short-term rise in share prices within a generally declining market.
- *Composite insurance issues:* the shares of general insurance companies (ie those that cover all types of risk – household, car, aviation, marine, etc) who also undertake life assurance.
- *Circular:* an analyst's report which includes his recommendation as to a particular share.
- *Thin market:* a market where there are few buyers or sellers. Prices in such a market tend to be more volatile as only a few transactions can significantly affect prices.
- *Oversold:* after a fall in a share's price as a result of some detrimental event or situation, there may be those who consider that the price is too low.

The *Daily Telegraph's* 'Tailpiece' is a popular part of the paper's market report. *The Independent* had a regular feature entitled 'Armchair Investment'. Although it tended to cover general matters as opposed to specific companies, it was nevertheless a very interesting column. Recommendations or share tips are also included in other papers. Some of the Sunday newspapers tip shares on a regular basis. On Mondays these are sometimes reported in the financial pages of the dailies.

However, it is not only share prices and tips which you should look out for in the daily financial pages; for example, the following extract from *The Independent* brings home the fact that small shareholdings are uneconomic to both investors and companies.

BOC cuts sale fee

Industrial gas company BOC has arranged a scheme allowing its small shareholders to sell their holdings without incurring full dealing charges. . . . Commonly brokers charge 1.65 per cent or a minimum fee, sometimes as much as £40. Private investors with less than 100 shares will have to be prepared to sell their entire holding if they use the scheme.

If BOC's share price on 19 March is the same as its close yesterday, 537p, someone with 100 shares will receive £537 less the 0.5 per cent commission (£2.68), or £534.32. . . .

BOC calculates that there are 3215 shareholders who own less than 100 shares. However, they command just 0.0272 per cent of BOC's total issued equity.

BOC said the scheme was set up in response to letters from small shareholders indicating their frustration of owning shares which they could not sell without incurring heavy charges.

The cost of sending annual reports and other paraphernalia to shareholders does not come cheap, especially in relation to the value of shares held by the smaller private investor.

So to give the smallest of shareholders an exit route is at least as much sense to the company as it is to the private investor.

The Independent, 15 February 1990

The papers also report economic news. Government statistics are reported and discussed. These include the Retail Price Index (RPI) published by the Department of Employment. This Index is based on a weighted basket of items which represent the cost of living. The RPI is compared to the previous month's and to past levels, so it gives an indication of the rate of inflation. Not only can the index be compared to inflation rates elsewhere in the world – a factor which is important to exporters and importers – but can also be regarded as the basis for real wage growth.

The Retail Sales Index (RSI) published by the Department of Trade not only reveals whether the volume and value of retail trade is declining, static or rising, but also indicates important trends in the level of consumer credit, which in turn reveals inflationary trends. An indicator of future retail prices are the two indices of producer prices published by the Department of Trade and Industry, which show costs and output prices for manufacturing concerns. Eventually, increases will find their way to the High Street.

The interpretation of all the statistical information available requires complex analysis. The papers give their views in City editorials or in separate features. Their own analysis is supplemented by the views of economists from the City institutions with the objective of giving a consensus opinion. Periodically the views of organisations such as the Institute for Fiscal Studies are given.

Some of the statistical data has a more obvious effect on certain sectors than others. For example, a decline in retail sales is clearly going to affect the stores sector and a decline in housing starts will mean lower profits for builders and those supplying building materials. The following extract also highlights the human factor in economic news – when employees are made redundant:

Building suppliers cut back as rates hit home

The number of new home starts slumped by 53,600 to fewer than 192,000 last year, down from 245,000 in 1988, as mortgage interest rates rose to crisis levels, the Environment Department said yesterday.

The situation worsened at the end of the year, with starts in the final quarter down by 34 per cent on a year earlier.

Redundancies include 482 at London Brick, 300 at Redland Tiles and more than 1000 at builders' merchants.

Last year's housing figures, still provisional, were the worst since 1982. The number of private homes started dipped by 51,800 to fewer than 165,000. Local authorities began only 13,600 down from 16,500. But housing associations – also regarded as 'public sector' – increased their starts from 12,600 to 13,700.

Some in the construction industry forecast that council house building will fall to fewer than 5000 a year under Government policies.

Brick stocks are soaring, with sales down by 26 per cent in the final quarter of last year, compared with a year earlier. Output was

more than a billion bricks, but only just over 800m were delivered.
Daily Telegraph, 6 February 1990

However, it is company news that is likely to be of the greatest interest to shareholders. This takes many different forms. A retailing group may announce an expansion programme; a computer manufacturer may unveil a new piece of equipment which will revolutionise the office, or a word processor which will be available at a previously unavailable low price – both announcements will potentially increase sales and hopefully profits, provided a rival company does not offer a comparable piece of equipment shortly afterwards; the launch of a new drug will enhance its manufacturer's prospects, but possibly hit the profitability of a rival; while the securing of a major account by an advertising agency could well mean higher profits, provided that it does not lose another customer. The reporting of company news and its impact on the current or future share price is a little like a game of snakes and ladders. Some announcements will send the investor up the rungs of the ladder, while others will result in a slide down a snake.

Shareholders will also be interested in company results. Those who are prudent will not just follow the companies in which they have shares, but will also note the progress of other companies in the same sector. After all, one company may be performing well at the expense of another, so never have a narrow view of the market.

The larger companies tend to publish their results in advertisements in the financial pages. These generally take the form of a brief resumé of their figures – turnover, profits before and after tax, earnings per share. Comparative figures are generally given for the previous reporting period. Key highlights from the Chairman's statement may also be given. However, the view of the market is more significant than the company's own opinion of its progress. It is not possible for every newspaper to analyse the results of every company in depth, so smaller companies may merely have a summary of their results reported under 'Company Results' with no comment accompanying the figures. On the other hand, the figures may be mentioned in a newspaper's market report. The impact on the share price could be accompanied by a brief comment such as, 'profits were below expectation', 'the figures were as analysts expected', or, 'the results took the City by surprise', or the reporter may elaborate further.

If a large company has reported, the figures will be considered to warrant more column inches. As the balance of the market report would be affected if an analysis was undertaken there, a more detailed study will appear elsewhere. It could be in the editorial, a news feature, or in the newspaper's share comment feature – for example, the *Financial Times'* 'Lex Column', the *Daily Telegraph's* 'Questor', *The Independent's* 'View from the City Road' or *The Time's* 'Tempus'. These columns are written by experienced journalists.

As well as having their own knowledge upon which to draw, the writers of these columns will be able to consult their paper's own records regarding the company and, most importantly, they will know where to go in the City for informed comment. They will talk to analysts and marketmakers as well as the company's executives at the press conference at which the results were announced. Their column will be a balanced view of the City's reaction to the results. However, it must be stressed that one paper's view may not be exactly the same as another. Some journalists, in the limited space available, will concentrate on some particular aspect considered to be of fundamental importance, while another will slant his piece in a slightly different direction. However, unless the City is split regarding the interpretation of the results, the general conclusions will not be poles apart.

In Chapter 1, the reporting of the plunge of the world's stock markets in October 1989 was examined. The event was triggered by a consortium, bidding with British Airways (BA) for United Airlines, failing to secure the required financing. It was the fact that the consortium (and not BA) was financing its bid by borrowing US$4.2bn which unsettled the banks. However, how did British Airways fare after the event? Here is an extract from *The Independent's* 'View from City Road' analysing BA's profits for the third quarter ending December 1989.

BA remains in holding pattern

British Airways is locked in something of a holding pattern at the moment. Increased revenue yields are being offset to a large extent by rising costs. The upshot is that BA's underlying trading profit is showing very little growth. So the company has to rely on the likes of aircraft disposals and pension contribution holidays for its profit increases.

BA argues such items are recurring and therefore constitute a genuine part of the continuing business. That would be a more acceptable argument if they were supplementing rather than providing profits growth. . . .

If demand was to tail off significantly, it would put even more pressure on the company to keep its costs under control and improve its margins. Neither is easy. . . .

It is easy to paint a gloomy picture for BA. However, when the company is viewed in the context of the global sector it becomes a more attractive proposition. KLM, its Dutch partner in the joint venture with Sabena, Belgium's national carrier, recently produced rather drab figures, and the US domestic airlines are very much out of favour.

BA has a strong US following which has lent considerable support to the share price. But if the transatlantic investors' enthusiasm for the stock is dulled by the poor outlook for the industry as a whole, then BA's price will begin to suffer. In the short term then, the prospects for the shares, down 2p at 196p, are not bright. Those who have supported the stock since it came to the market three years ago this week at 120p have no reason to sell. However, there is no incentive to buy just yet, and better opportunities will present themselves.

The Independent, 15 February 1990

Takeovers

Introduction

The juiciest news in the City relates to bids by one giant company for another. If the figures concerned are large or the bid emotive, for example when a foreign company bids for an established British institution, not only will the takeover result in headlines in the financial pages, but as we saw in Chapter 1 when Ford bid for Jaguar, every national newspaper considers the news worthy of banner headlines on their front pages.

It may come as a surprise to those who do not closely follow the financial press to learn that bids and mergers (the agreement of two companies to combine for their mutual benefit) are almost daily occurrences. The majority, while important to the parties concerned, are not considered of national importance and receive scant newspaper coverage, if any at all. It may be that a local limited company which is not quoted on the stock market, bids for another family-run limited company in the vicinity. Even takeovers by some companies which are quoted on the Stock Exchange only receive a passing mention in the financial press. Generally, it is only when a giant bids for another company of stature that the market and the press become excited.

Why a company makes a bid

The predator company stalks its victim in the belief that the acquisition will benefit its business. Naturally, there will be certain economic factors such as a more economical distribution network, economies of scale and management rationalisation if both companies are in the same or a similar line of business. However, in such situations, there is always the risk that the Government may be concerned that a monopoly will be created. Consequently, the bid, or a merger, may be referred to the Monopolies and Mergers Commission (MMC). This could delay matters for six months or more while the situation is investigated. The referral may prove unfounded, or, faced with the delay, the predator company may decide to abandon its bid. All the investor can do if an MMC investigation is considered likely, is read the press comment and make up his mind whether to sell the holding in the victim company or to wait until the result of the referral is announced. Even if there is a negative response from the MMC, or even before its deliberations are announced, a new predator may emerge.

The parties to a bid do not necessarily have to be in the same line of business. The bidder may decide that the industry in which it is involved is in decline and the diversification into another field is the order of the day. On the other hand, it may consider growth by acquisition to be quicker than organic growth. Whatever its reason, its objective will be to increase its return on capital. Whether this will be achieved will only be revealed in the future.

The market may feel that its management is entering into unknown territory. If the market is not convinced about the benefits of the proposed bid, the demand for the predator's shares could decline. Where supply exceeds demand, the price of the predator company's shares could fall. Indeed, this may occur in any situation, not just takeovers for the purpose of diversification or growth. If the market does not believe that the predator company will enhance its situation if the bid materialises, generally its share price will fall.

Not all takeovers have the intention of integrating two companies. The bidder may be interested in certain of its victim's activities, but not in others. The bid may be made with the intention of retaining the core business, but selling off certain subsidiaries at a later date. Indeed, it is not unknown for a successful bidder to hive off certain companies within the group acquired, for more than was paid for the whole. Admittedly this is more difficult now than in the past. In the 1950s and 1960s fortunes were amassed by asset-strippers – individuals or corporate entities which made bids for companies and then resold their land, buildings and other assets which were grossly undervalued in their balance sheets.

The advantages of a bid to shareholders in victim companies

Having looked briefly at why a bidder considers it will benefit from a takeover, it is now time to examine the benefits for shareholders in the victim company. In Chapter 1, the Jaguar–Ford story was unfolded by way of extracts from the press in September 1989. A brief resumé is appropriate here.

On 1 September, the share price was 415p. The year's 'High-Low' was 424p–264p. In the middle of the month, the company declared a pre-tax profit of £1.4m and an operating loss of £2.8m, which was far short of the City's pre-tax profit forecast of £8m. At the time, Mr Stephen Reitman, analyst of UBS Phillips & Drew commented, 'The profits this year were of academic interest except in that they underline the problems of currency. [The majority of Jaguar's sales are to the US.] Even then they increase the prospects of a takeover attempt.' This was reported in the *Financial Times* market report on 14 September. It also revealed that dealers suggested Ford as a possible suitor. Three days later, the *Sunday Times* ran a story revealing that Jaguar was looking towards a partnership with GM. On 19 September 1989, Ford made a pre-emptive bid for a minority stake in Jaguar. The company's share price rose to 467p. By the end of the month, Jaguar's shares were 572p.

Speculation continued throughout October 1989 against the background of the Government's golden share, which limited bidders to a 14.9 per cent stake until 1 January 1991. However, on 2 November 1989, the Government announced that it was waiving its golden share. Ford make a £1.6bn bid for Jaguar equivalent to 850p per share. Jaguar's shares had therefore doubled in the space of two months and had increased more than threefold from its low of the year. Although Ford paid 850p per share, the price had been higher before the announcement.

There were no counter-bids. Founder shareholders who secured Jaguar shares in August 1984 at 165p had to be content with just over a fivefold increase in value in as many years.

Spotting a likely victim

Most shareholders would like to enjoy the windfall of their shares being the subject to a bid by another company. This is especially so when the offer is well above the current share price. It is therefore not surprising that the very whiff of a possible bid raises the adrenalin a point or two. The following extract from the *Daily Telegraph's* 'Market Report' of 6 September 1989 illustrates the excitement that even the most unfounded of rumours can generate. It is stressed that this piece is exceptional, for on the previous day speculation was rife across all sectors regarding possible takeovers:

Mega-bid buzz spurs equities

London markets were given a late boost by excited speculation that this morning could witness another mega takeover bid.

The main gossip was in the brewery sector where American demand for **Allied-Lyons**, long suggested as a potential break-up target, saw the bears running for cover; the shares ended 11 up to a high of 566p, capitalising the group at £4.27bn.

Guinness also attracted the punters and closed 7 better at 604p.

Early in the day, shares were looking tired and dealers used professional profit-taking to partly square their books.

However, the subsequent bounce proved that there was still plenty of life in the market and the long-established FT-30 Share Index posted a record with a rise of 5.0 to 2008.6.

The wider-based FT 100 Index, down 8.8 around noon, closed 6.8 better at a post-crash high of 2426.0; the best ever level for this measurement was 2443.4 on July 16, 1987. . . .

Keep an eye on **Yale & Valor**, 347p, was the chatter around the market. Michael Montague's security and home products group, whose bid for Myson, subsequently rivalled by Blue Circle Industries, now rests with the Monopolies Commission, is said itself to be a likely bid target.

Some say that Nigel Rudd's industrial conglomerate Williams Holdings, which owns a 5.85pc stake in Y&V, could increase its holding preparatory to a full-scale offer. . . .

Amersham International, all the rage on Monday following a resurgence of bid speculation, quickly ran into profit-taking and reacted 27 to 467p. . . .

Dealers were intrigued by a market put-through of a new 3 per cent stake in Caird Group, the waste disposal company which recently took a 4.7pc holding in the fellow waste disposal business, Leigh Interests. The put-through, believed to have gone from an institutional holder to a non-institutional buyer, raised the question about possible takeover interest. **Caird** shares hardened to 546p. . . .

  Ocean Transport, a strong market on Monday on hopes of a bid from 27.5pc stakeholder Sir Ron Brierley improved 7 more to 375p. **Armstrong Equipment**, where Caparo Group has failed to find a buyer for its 29.5pc stake at the minimum tender price of 185p, rallied 6 to 169p as institutional supporters came on the scene. . . .

Daily Telegraph, 6 September 1989

The million dollar question is, 'How does the investor know which shares to buy in order to benefit from being a shareholder in the Victim Company?' Unfortunately, there is no way that such events can be predicted with any degree of certainty. The experienced punter on the stock market has a similar degree of knowledge as to each company's form. He will know their history, their performance records against good, bad and indifferent economic backgrounds and the expertise of their management team. The punter in the takeover stakes will be on the lookout for lame ducks which have potential.

This does not mean that they are on the lookout for companies which are about to sink into oblivion. Instead, they search for solid companies which are of long-term value, but which, for various reasons, are either performing badly or have a management team that is somewhat undynamic. On the other hand, it may be a company, which while profitable, has been underperforming its sector for some time. The reasons why some companies catch the eye of those on the lookout for likely victims of predators are varied. However, the common theme is that under different management the company's full potential can be exploited.

This is only one real criterion that those in the takeover stakes are looking for. A company may be considered ripe for a bid if its share value is below its net asset value per share. For example, the company may have undeveloped land in its balance sheet which is valued as 'industrial', but which has potential for being developed for residential housing. This is an example of a situation of a company not exploiting its full potential. Another approach is to identify companies which are on the lookout for acquisitions and attempt to 'stand in their shoes' and put yourself in the situation of those looking for likely victims and acquire a holding in companies for which they may make a bid.

An alternative is to scan the financial press for ideas. Do not act on every tip you read, otherwise you will soon find yourself short of funds. It is essential to analyse all the situations and to make up your own mind. Certain companies are periodically tipped as takeover victims for years and nothing happens. Others who realise they are vulnerable to predators take action, such as a liaison with another company. For example, Pearson plc, the conglomorate whose interests range from the *Financial Times* to Madame Tussauds and which embraces a wide range of publishing interests as well as Lazards the merchant bankers, was subject to speculative talk in the 1980s as its net asset value was considered by some to be far above its market capitalisation. There was press comment that lawyers employed by unknown persons were considering how to unlock these assets. The matter was complicated by a complex share structure. Speculative talk was effectively quashed in 1988 when the company formed a liaison with the Dutch company Elsevier by means of a share swap.

Read the financial press and note their comments regarding likely bids. Provided you invest in solid companies and do not buy purely because of takeover speculation, you could reap rewards when a bid does materialise. However, patience is required – and a certain degree of luck. Above all, do not acquire non-voting shares, or shares which are closely held either by family members of the founder or others because you will not be able to vote when important issues concerning the company arise. Trusthouse Forte's long, contracted and unsuccessful battle for Savoy Hotels is a good example of this situation.

The terms of the offer

Rumours aside, the first indication that something is afoot can be a brief announcement by either the predator company or the victim, or indeed a joint statement, that a bid has been made or received and that the parties are now talking. Alternatively, the Stock Exchange may suspend the company's share quote, either at the request of both parties or following an unexplained price movement in the shares of the victim company. It is a requirement that when a single buyer, which includes arrangements where two or more buyers act together (called a 'concert party'), acquire a shareholding over 5 per cent in a company, the holding has to be announced. At the time this information is published, it may be accompanied by a brief statement of intention. This may indicate whether the holding is an 'investment' or whether a future bid may be planned.

The victim company can reject the offer outright, declaring that the terms are unacceptable. Alternatively, it may announce that it will be studying the terms of the offer and reject or accept the terms at a later date. A rejection can lead to a war being mounted between the two companies. The victim company will set out its reasons, sometimes in the strongest of terms, as to why the bid is rejected. Needless to say, the predator company will put its views forward in equally strong terms as to why the offer should be accepted by the victim company's shareholders.

Public relation consultants may be employed and costly persuasion campaigns launched. Both companies will write to the victim company's shareholders, press and TV advertising may be used and meetings may be held with those who hold large blocks of shares. At the peak of the campaigns one cannot help wondering whether it would not be better for the parties to devote the same strenuous efforts in the direction of running their companies.

In addition to impassioned and vitriolic language, some of the statements made by both parties can tend towards the libellous. The proceedings are watched by the Panel on Takeovers and Mergers (see page 77), which can intervene if matters get out of hand. The situation can really get lively when a third party enters the takeover stakes. If the original bid was unwanted (referred to as 'hostile'), the victim company may invite a company it would like to be conquered by to make a counter-bid. Such a bidder is called a 'white knight'.

The whole affair can turn into a very dramatic soap opera. Read the advertisements and the circulars that pop through your letter-box and follow the press comment. The most important piece of paper you will receive is the offer document sent by the company making the bid. This not only sets out the terms and conditions of the offer, but also contains a considerable amount of information regarding both companies so that shareholders can assess the bid. The Panel on Takeovers and Mergers, which administers the City Code on takeovers and mergers, insists on full and accurate information being included in offer documents. Profit forecasts must be approved by qualified accountants; assets must be valued by independent professionals and the basis of the valuation clearly indicated (eg a going concern, break-up value, etc); if there is an element of a cash offer, confirmation is required that the funds are available.

Thankfully, the main points are summarised. If the offer is accepted by the victim company, a letter will accompany the offer document stating that the terms have been approved by its merchant bankers. If the offer has not been accepted, there will be comment in the financial press which will help you to decide what action to take. If you are in any doubt as to what to do, consult your stockbroker or financial adviser for guidance. Remember that the bidder will write about the financial implications of the bid in glowing terms.

Obviously, the terms of the offer are important. It may take various forms, for example:

- a straight cash bid;
- an offer of shares in the company making the bid;
- a mixture of cash and shares;
- a choice of shares or cash;
- an offer of convertible or fixed loan stock in the company making the bid;
- the offer of a mixture of shares and fixed loan stock in the company making the bid;
- a mixture of shares, fixed loan stock and cash.

Most bids include a cash alternative. However, it must be remembered that the acceptance of cash is the same as selling your shares and this could, according to your personal circumstances, result in a capital gains tax liability. Consult your tax adviser if you are in any doubt. The acceptance of shares, convertible or fixed loan stock, is a straightforward exchange of securities and is viewed by the Inland Revenue as a continuation of the existing investment and consequently there are no capital gains tax implications until the new securities are realised. If accepting securities, clearly the opinion as to the potential of the new combined company is of prime importance. Watch out for comment in the financial press.

It must be pointed out that offers are always conditional. Generally, they are dependent upon the bid not being referred to the Monopolies and Mergers Commission and the International Stock Exchange granting a listing for the new securities being issued. It is easy to overlook one hurdle that has to be crossed – the approval of the bid by the bidder company's own shareholders. Naturally, the offer will also be conditional upon a given proportion of shareholders accepting the offer. This is usually anything from 51 to 90 per cent.

The required action

Having weighed up all the pros and cons and decided whether to take the cash alternative or shares, or a mixture of the two, it is time for action. An alternative is to sell the shares (see page 116). However, if accepting the offer it would be unwise to react immediately. The offer document will give precise instructions as to what action is required. It is simply a case of indicating whether you are accepting cash, securities or a combination of the two, signing the form and returning it with the share certificate relating to your holding in the company which is the subject of the bid to a stated address. The latest date for acceptances will be clearly indicated.

Is there any reason to delay completing the form? Quite simply, yes, a better offer may materialise or a counter-bid may be made by a third party. Delaying the posting of your completed acceptance until two to three days before the deadline will not go amiss. In the event of postal delays, late acceptances will generally not be turned away if the offer is declared unconditional. Of course, if a better offer emerges before the deadline, it would not be prudent to accept the first one.

The Panel of Takeovers and Mergers

The Panel of Takeovers and Mergers protects the interests of shareholders. Although the panel's city code on takeovers does not have the force of law, those who do not follow its guidelines are likely to be ostracised by the City. The Panel has the power to ask the International Stock Exchange to suspend price quotations during a bid and to refuse listings for new securities that the bid company proposes to issue as part of its bid. These sanctions are perhaps more effective than the force of law. The Panel also restricts the number of shares that a predator may acquire in a 'dawn raid'. This is a single operation to secure shares in the market and/or from institutions. It is generally conducted early in the day, hence dawn raid. This practice made the headlines in the early 1980s. Dawn raids have not actually been banned, but bidders must now restrict themselves to securing only 14.9 per cent of the victim's share capital in this way. After a moratorium of a week, which is a period in which others can assess the situation, the bidder can enter the market again. However, when a holding reaches 30 per cent of the share capital of the victim company, a bid must be made for the remaining shares. The bid price must be no less than the 'high price' in the market over the past 12 months. There are various other rules aimed at protecting shareholders, including the acquisition of shares by a group of parties acting in concert – a concert party.

Points to note

When a bid is in the offing, or indeed, after it has been made, your shares can be sold at any time. Before a bid has been made, you may already consider that the share price has been driven up to a level which you find tempting. Of course, the price in the future could be more beneficial, but on occasion you may prefer a bird in the hand rather than two in the bush. Theoretically a stake of 29.9 per cent of a company's shareholding can be built up without the stakeholder having to make a bid, but it is unusual for nothing to happen when a decent proportion of shares have been secured.

Investors who like to speculate on the takeover stakes, purchase shares in companies in situations where there is a fair following wind for a bid being made. In the Jaguar situation, those who purchased when there were the first rumours of a likely takeover would have more than doubled their money. However, remember that many of the rumours remain just that, perhaps for ever.

After a bid has been made, do not forget to monitor the victim company's share price. If a cash offer has been made, do not be surprised if the price of its shares in the market is below the offer figure. This simply reflects that investors have discounted the receipt of a certain sum at some later time. The concept of 'discounting' is simple. What would you prefer, £100 now or £100 in the future? The answer is, of course, the former. Indeed, most individuals would accept slightly less money now rather than wait a few weeks. This is because the sum received now can immediately be put to work. In other words, it could be placed on deposit and possibly earn more than the 'discount' – ie the difference between the sum to be paid in the future and the slightly smaller amount to be received immediately.

However, if the offer solely comprises securities issued by the predator company, and if the victim company's share price is below the value of the bid, it could well be that the market is a little concerned about the value of the predator company's paper. In other words, it may consider that the terms are too generous and that the price of the predator company's shares will be lower after the companies are amalgamated, compared to before the bid. If it is considered that '2 + 2' will make less than 4, the market for victim company's shares may be difficult after the bid has been finalised. There is a lower risk of a difficult market in the shares of the bidder company, if the company for which it is bidding is smaller than itself. The press will comment on the virtues of takeovers both from the viewpoint of the bidder and the company for which it is bidding. Take note of what is written. Perhaps you may decide it is better to opt out.

This advice is equally applicable to shareholders in the predator company. If you spot the signs, either by lower share prices being quoted in the share prices page of your newspaper or reports of uncertainty regarding the merits of the takeover, carefully consider your position and consult your financial adviser if you are in doubt.

If you are opposed to the takeover, do not run the risk of becoming a minority shareholder, who neither accepts the offer nor 'sells out'. Of course, the opposition to a bid may be so strong that it is apparent that it will not materialise. However, should holders of at least 90 per cent of a company's share capital accept the bid, then the predator company can notify dissenting shareholders within four months that it will compulsorily purchase their shares on the same terms before two months have elapsed.

It has already been stated that an offer is usually conditional upon a certain proportion of acceptances being received. This can be anything from 51 to 90 per cent of the total share capital. Should this not be achieved, all those who accepted will have their share certificates returned. However, in the event of the level of acceptances achieved to make the offer unconditional being less than 90 per cent, the dissenting shareholders could find themselves in an awkward situation. The market for their shares may be small. If this is the case, it will possibly be difficult to sell their shares. This will be especially so if the shares of the predator company have not performed well.

Takeovers add spice to the stock market. However, do not expect every rumour of a bid or takeover tip to materialise. The takeover stakes requires patience and a certain degree of luck as well.

4

Tipsters, Newsletters and Magazines

'The gambling known as business looks with austere disfavour upon the business known as gambling' Ambrose Bierce. Quoted HL Mencken

Introduction

There is a bewildering amount of written information available concerning shares, unit trusts, investment trusts, gilts and other investment possibilities. If the potential investor were to wade through all the advice, tips and suggestions, he would have no time available to decide which would be the most suitable home for his capital. Self-selection is certainly not for those who find making a choice difficult.

It is not surprising that many individuals choose to use the services of an adviser. If it later proves that the professional's advice was not as good as it could have been, at least there may be some comfort in the fact that the experts were consulted. On the other hand, there may be a nagging feeling that the choice of adviser was not quite right. Hindsight provides no comfort.

However, even if you do decide to take advice from a stockbroker or other professional, there is no excuse for being completely clueless as to the investment possibilities. A little knowledge can be a dangerous thing, but on the other hand, it could guide you away from investments that a professional may recommend. Although under the Financial Services Act, those offering financial counselling should give 'best advice', there is no guarantee that what they consider 'best' actually *is* best. Professionals are not infallible, nor are investors. So, a reasonable knowledge of financial matters can be viewed as an investor's safety net. Where does the potential investor start researching?

A good start would be a look at the market reports and comment found on the financial pages of quality newspapers which were examined in Chapter 3. However, there are other sources of information which may influence you in deciding whether to make a particular investment.

Tips

A tip you are given in a pub or at some other social gathering to buy a particular company's shares ranks alongside a tip on a horse in the reliability stakes. Some may prove to be absolute winners, others may fall at the first fence. Treat casual tips such as these with scepticism.

Tips also appear in the popular publications with little or no explanation as to why the shares are being recommended. Only be tempted to follow these hunches if they are accompanied by a logical explanation as to why the shares should be added to your portfolio. One favourite ploy in the past was for a journalistic tipster to recommend a share which he knew was tightly held. Perhaps a large proportion of the shares were in the hands of the family of the company's founders, in various trusts, etc. Whatever the reason, he knew that there was only a limited supply available in the market. Only a slight increase in the demand for the shares would increase the price. How gratifying to write up the success of his tip two or three weeks later!

Never buy or sell shares on what purports to be 'inside' information from relatives, friends or acquaintances. If the 'hot tip' does not transpire to be from a source close to the company, the information could at best prove to be unprofitable and at worst disastrous. Should the 'hot tip' be a result of 'inside' information, it could result in criminal proceedings. Although 'insider dealing' is a term which refers to directors, key employees and a company's advisers, the definition legally embraces anyone who acts on privileged information used before an official announcement. You have been warned.

Newsletters

When the stock market is booming, those newsletters which are forwarded to subscribers for an annual fee, appear to mushroom. When I asked a stockbroker what he thought of such publications, he replied, 'Why pay for the privilege of losing money?' Although this comment does injustice to those long-established and reputable newsletters which contain information based on careful research and analysis, it does highlight the fact that some are positively dubious. With desk-top publishing, or a word processor, such newsletters are cheap to produce and the potential rewards for the publishers high.

So, are newsletters a good source of information for the possible purchase of shares by the small investor? You will have to make up your own mind. However, it does seem a little pointless to pay a large subscription for a skimpy publication, when for a much lower sum, you can subscribe to a good weekly publication which covers a much broader spectrum containing financial news generally, company results and ideas for possible investments.

There is another point to consider. Unless you have sufficient funds to play the market on a regular basis, there is the temptation, when bombarded with a whole list of 'make-it-rich-quick' tips to begin to buy uneconomic parcels of shares. In other words, by making purchases of a few hundred pounds of shares at a time. With minimum dealing costs of £20 to £30 or more, acquiring the holding and realising the profit could cost more than £60. An investment of, say, £250, would have to increase by around 20 per cent before the dealing costs could be covered. It is far better to acquire a few decent holdings rather than a number of small parcels of shares. If your objective is to spread the risk of share ownership, consider investing in unit trusts.

Stockbrokers' newsletters

Most stockbrokers issue regular publications for their clients. These vary from a broadsheet comprising a single folded sheet of A3 to an A4 booklet. Some are written with the small investor in mind, while others are more sophisticated and intended for the more experienced investor.

A typical format for the broadsheets might be a general market round-up analysed against the economic background. This may be followed by a feature covering a particular sector of the market. A forthcoming privatisation may warrant a special article, with the future prospects of the particular company being explored in depth. The plus and minus factors of investing in the forthcoming issue will be highlighted and general advice given as to the market's likely reaction to the flotation at a range of prices. Acccording to the publication date *vis-à-vis* the issue, specific advice may be given to potential investors.

A section may be devoted to general personal financial matters. This will generally embrace the 'flavours of the month', for example, what action to take on the advent of independent taxation. The approach of a budget may result in an article on an investment vehicle currently enjoying tax concessions which the Chancellor may axe. On the other hand, the Government may have enhanced a particular investment scheme, for example, personal equity plans were made more attractive by the 1989 Budget. Financial planning may also be covered. For example, a feature on inheritance tax may highlight the effects on the average estate in order to focus the reader's mind on the problems that could be faced by his heirs.

Not all subjects covered will be investment orientated. For example, the merits or otherwise of equity release schemes, whereby the elderly can release capital from their largest asset, their home, may be examined. The possibilities are endless.

The final sections of the broadsheets are generally devoted to recommended buys. Certain brokers also include recommended sells or shares which should be 'held', ie retained if they are in your portfolio, but not to be purchased if they are not. The 'buy', 'sell' or 'hold' recommendations are accompanied by brief details. An example might be:

> A small, growing company with superb potential. It has combined a series of sensible acquisitions with a strengthening management team. Net borrowing is only around £2.3m, which is about 9 per cent gearing.

Gilts may be recommended for growth, others for income. Unit trusts are also not forgotten. The recommendations are a result of the stockbroker's research. In addition to the financial information available, they will analyse the company against the sector. If there has been an acquisition, the enhancements to profits will be analysed not only against projections for the future, but also with regard to anticipated economies made by streamlined distribution networks, the bulk purchase of raw materials and management economies. As already mentioned in Chapter 1, stockbrokers benefit from presentations by companies of their future plans and prospects. They analyse what they learn and publish their views.

The 'weightier' newsletters, which are written for those investors with large portfolios, naturally go into greater depth. In fact, those who publish their research in booklet form, would probably object to the term 'newsletter', for certainly they are in a different category to broadsheets. Furthermore, they are likely to be published more frequently than monthly. For example, Greenwell Montagu's *Market Focus* is published for each account period. The edition published on 26 January 1990 for the account commencing 29 January and ending on 9 February had this to say about Allied-Lyons:

Meeting with Richard Martin, Chief Executive of Allied-Lyons on Monday 22nd January 1990.

The tone of the meeting was quietly positive, which is at odds with the share price which has looked pretty depressed since mid-summer. There are, however, a number of reasons for the disappointing share price.

Firstly, Mr Alan Bond, the Australian entrepreneur, has finally gone away, his tail between his legs and the one-time 10 per cent stake disposed of. Secondly, the Monopolies Commission report on the tied house system has found against the major brewers and requires them to sell some of their houses. Also, Allied is in the course of several deals, changing the emphasis of the business.

In the last three months it has bought Dunkin Donuts in the US for £200m and Whitbread's spirits division for some £550m, in moves which will increase its borrowing substantially. It proposes to sell Embassy Hotels – perhaps for £300m.

After these deals, Allied will be strongly represented in internationally known brands, eg Skol, Castlemaine lagers, Harvey's wines, Beefeater gin, Long John and Cutty Sark whisky, Bollinger champagne, Tetley tea, Lyons cakes. Its profits will be derived, roughly, 50 per cent wines or spirits, 25 per cent beer and 25 per cent from food. Growth in earnings, though modest in 1990, will be excellent in the longer term. We would buy these out of favour shares, yielding prospectively 4½ per cent at 500p.

Greenwell Montagu, *Market Focus*, 26 January 1990

(Note: This is historic advice. Research is an ongoing process and views can and do change in the light of developments which are either directly related to a company or the sector in which it is categorised.)

In addition to a stockbroker publishing in-depth research of particular companies, an 'at a glance' table may be published summarising its research department's views of a hundred or so companies which its analysts cover. This may include an 'indication of the share's anticipated growth potential'. For example, high, above, below, low average growth or, of course, average growth. In addition to the research recommendation, such as hold, sell or buy, the price may be given at a particular date together with yields and PE ratios.

These newsletters are issued free to clients. It must be noted that a stockbroker's recommendations are just that – statements that the shares are worthy, or otherwise, of purchase. In no way is it a guarantee for the future. Indeed, the newsletters contain caveats to this effect. Shares with a 'buy' indicator could flop, whereas those with a 'sell' recommendation may soar.

How reliable are newsletters? A study published in February 1990 by the Chicago-based Zacks Investment Research reported on the 'stock-picking prowess' of the cream of Wall Street's broking houses. The study estimated individual investors' total returns by tracking the stocks most recommended by each firm. According to the survey, shares tipped by nine of the ten major firms lost money in the last three months of 1989, despite each firm having a large research department.

During the period, the Dow Jones Index rose 3.2 per cent and the more broadly based Standard and Poors 500 Index increased by 2.1 per cent. The estimate of individual investors' returns had they followed the advice of one broker would have been a loss of 3.3 per cent, with losses in certain stocks recommended being as high as 50 per cent.

Taking the whole of 1989, the broking firms did not do much better. Only four of the top ten managed to out-perform the main indices. The worst performer of the top ten only managed a 19.8 per cent gain for the year, which was less than two-thirds of the rise in the Dow Jones in 1989. One director of research at the firm which came out on top commented to the *Daily Telegraph*, 'If you can't even track the main indexes then you should not be in this business. We have come out on top because we have good ideas and a first-rate team of analysts.' Not surprisingly, the broking houses were concerned at the poor level of research.

If the experts cannot get it right, what hope is there for the individual shareholder? Read newsletters by all means and be guided by their recommendations. However, do also read the financial pages in the national press and specialist periodicals and make your own judgement having digested the views from more than one source.

Specialist periodicals

In recent years there has been an increasing interest in personal finance and stockmarket investment. Not surprisingly, publishers have responded to the demand for information by providing new titles. This section takes a brief look at what is on offer.

Investors Chronicle

Incorporating *Investors Review* and *Financial World*, the *Investors Chronicle* is no newcomer. It is a long-established weekly published each Friday by FT Business Information Limited. It has a very good reputation and at £1.20 a copy (annual subscription £62), it represents excellent value for money. Special subscription offers are also available from time to time.

The section of most interest in the magazine to those on the lookout for an investment in shares is 'Tips of the Week'. It does not restrict itself to tipping 'buys' – it also recommends when it is time to sell a holding. Before giving examples of the presentation of the tips and the in-depth reporting on the companies recommended, it is essential to focus on the **warning** which features prominently on the magazine's title page. In addition to the usual caveats regarding the fluctuation of share prices, the possibility of the value of shares falling below the sum originally invested and the fact that some shares have a poor marketability (the magazine indicates the fact if this is the case), one paragraph is particularly pertinent to quoting past tips here. It reads, 'when considering investing it is advisable to ask whoever deals for you about marketability, *and remember that circumstances may change after our recommendations are published*' (author's emphasis). It must be stressed that the following extracts are purely illustrative of the *Investors Chronicle's* style and are historic.

TIPS OF THE WEEK

Beckenham
Ductwork for heating systems is Beckenham's main earner, and demand remains strong despite signs elsewhere of a construction downturn. Beckenham has some underused assets to sweat harder too, following the recent Bardsey purchase, and earnings are expected to rise by a fifth this time for a PE ratio of 8. Good value.

Securiguard
Security and cleaning contracting are steady businesses with little exposure to those parts of the economy clobbered by high interest rates. Securiguard has anyhow diversified into the US, helping lift earnings by almost a quarter last year. On a prospective PE ratio of 9 the shares are cheap.

Pentland

Pentland is still heavily dependent on its US sports shoe making associate Reebok. Reebok had a tricky 1988, but there are signs of a modest recovery. The dollar's improvement is another plus for Pentland, and on a PE ratio of just 6 the shares are worth punting on for further recovery possibilities.

FII-Fyffes

FII-Fyffes is an Irish based fruit and vegetable distributor, making most of its profits in the UK, where the trend towards better quality and higher margin produce is boosting profits. Earnings rose a fifth last time and with another good increase in sight the shares are solid value on a likely PE ratio of 11.

RCO

RCO is another small cleaning contractor, benefitting from contract renewals at reasonable margins, after cut throat competion in the initial battle for health service contracts left the pickings thin. The present wave of local authority contracts coming up for grabs will enlarge its marketplace, and the shares are solid value on a likely PE ratio of 10.

Berkeley Govett

Once a specialist in Californian high tech companies, Berkeley is now a far more broadly based fund manager. Buoyant stockmarkets meant a one quarter rise in earnings last year and Berkeley's long-run record is excellent. Worth buying on a PE ratio below 7.

Sock Shop

The well-known hosiery and sock retailer is yet another victim of the high street shakeout, warning of losses and the need for a cash injection. It's hard to see who'll cough up fresh funds at the current market price, and although the shares have already sunk a long way, investors should cut their losses and sell.

Investors Chronicle, 9–15 February 1990

(Note: Sock Shop's shares were suspended at 34p on 21 February 1990 prior to the company announcing it had asked for administrators to be appointed after failing to negotiate a re-financing package.)

The magazine's 'Companies' section elaborates further on the recommendations (the tips are cross-referenced to the relevant page). Here is further information on the above companies (the figures in brackets relate to the previous financial year):

BECKENHAM
Heating duct installer and tool distributor
Results for year to 31.10.89
Turnover: £77.7m (£46.0m) + 46%
Pre-tax profits: £3.82m (£2.17m) + 76%
Stated earnings: 8.9p (7.7p) + 16%
Final dividend: 1.5p (1.5p)
Share price: 86p   Mkt cap: £38.8m
1989–90 high: 116p   low: 72p
PE ratio: 10   Yield: 4.6%

The organic growth shown by these figures confirms Beckenham's claim that demand for ductwork (now a major proportion of the cost of a new building) remains strong. The company accompanied its August promotion to the USM with a one for three rights issue and its market value has subsequently been boosted by the largely paper-financed acquisition of tool distributor Bardsey.

Turnover this year is likely easily to pass the £100m mark, and brokers BZW are expecting profits to double to £7m if currently underused assets begin to sweat. Despite more equity, earnings will be enhanced by the acquisitions and the prospective PE ratio is 8. **Good value.**

SECURIGUARD
Security and cleaning contractor
Results for year to 5.5.89
Turnover: £104m (£51.1m) + 104%
Pre-tax profits: £6.22m (£3.22m) + 93%
Stated earnings: 24.6p (20.0p) + 23%
Share price: 286p   Mkt cap: £53.3m
1989–90 high: 299p   low: 199p
PE ratio: 13   Yield: 3.7%

All divisions performed well on margins of 6 per cent especially cleaning and maintenance, where profits nearly doubled. But gearing is high at 180 per cent – £359,000 was paid in interest, compared with £123,000 received last time. And further acquisitions in either security or cleaning are likely to be paper-funded. Following last month's acquisition of York-based Madison for up to £10.6m, US sales should be nearly a third of the whole next year, compared to less than a fifth now. Pointing to the stock's good defensive qualities, BZW are looking for £9.1m pre-tax this year for a prospective PE of 9. **That's cheap on fundamentals.**

PENTLAND
Reebok leaps ahead

The fortunes of consumer products group Pentland are closely tied to those of the US sports shoe maker Reebok, in which it has a 32 per cent stake. So Pentland shares edged ahead on news of good 1989 profits from its associate. These came in ahead of expectations at £178m), on sales of 1.12bn (£1.01bn).

Reebok has recovered from a difficult 1988, thanks to substantial R&D investment. This has led to new products such as the air-filled pump, which, in turn, have given Reebok a boost in the fashion stakes and strengthened the brand as a whole.

Pentland, which has also benefited from the strength of the dollar against sterling, depends on Reebok for around four-fifths of its profits. When its own 1989 figures are released in March, joint company brokers Warburg are looking for pre-tax profits of £70m, against a restated £59.7m in 1988. With Pentland's shares on 83p, the prospective PE is 7. **Solid value.**

FII-FYFFES
Fruit and vegetable distributor

Results for year to 31.10.89
Turnover: IR£413m (IR£293m) + 41%
Pre-tax profits: IR£525.0m (IR£19.1m) + 31%
Stated earnings: 6.21IRp (5.13IRp) + 21%
Final dividend: 0.67IRp (0.61IRp) + 10%
Share price: 116IRp   Mkt cap: IR £342m
1989–90 high: 116IRp   low: 74IRp
PE ratio: 14   Yield: 1.0%

(Note: IR£ = Irish Republic £; IRp = Irish Republic pence.)

Around 70 per cent of operating profits come from UK and Fyffes' decision to translate them at year end rates meant that weakening sterling took around 7 per cent off the bottom line. On the other hand, rising interest rates have been mighty helpful to a company with IR£60m in the bank and with another IR£25m likely to be generated in the current year.

Acquisitions have put in a position to fight it out with Geest in the UK, and its first European purchase is eagerly awaited. Declan Magee at brokers Riada has pencilled in IR£30m for 1990. The prospective PE ratio is 12 with the share price soft ahead of some continental news. **Solid value.**

RCO
Cleaning Contractor

Results for year to 30.9.89
Turnover: £28.9m (£22.5m) + 28%

Pre-tax profits: £2.89m (£2.01m) + 44%
Stated earnings: 17.3p (12.1p) + 43%
Final dividend: 5.4p (4.0p) + 35%
Share price: 225p   Mkt cap: £23.8m
1989–1990 high: 225p   low: 125p
PE ratio: 13   Yield: 4.8%

RCO has been one of the major beneficiaries of increased compulsory tendering and contracting out by public bodies. It was deliberately a little slow to jump into the battle for NHS contracts a couple of years ago and since then has been able to pick up Health Service work on better margins. The same process may be repeated with the local authorities. In both cases though the institutions are now contracting out many services other than cleaning and RCO is broadening its operations to match. Brokers Kleinwort Benson forecast current year profits up another 20 per cent at £3.5m, implying a prospective PE ratio of 10. **Solid value.**

BERKELEY GOVETT
Strong progress
Buoyant world stockmarkets and the success of its funds for investing in fashionable markets on the Pacific rim gave Jersey-based fund manager Berkeley Govett a successful 1989. Pre-tax profits, earnings per share and the final dividend all rose by a quarter to $39.3m, 42c and 10c respectively.

The UK arm, John Govett, now manages over £2bn in funds (compared with £1.6bn a year ago), and as long as there's not another crash, that figure will keep growing. In addition, this year should see profits starting to flow from the US life insurance company Berkeley set up last year. It lost about $1.5m in 1989, but is 'doing wonderfully' in terms of bringing in premium income.

The corporate finance operation has a less exciting (if still 'quite good') outlook, and Berkeley's involvement in 'mezzanine finance' – that's junk bonds to you and me – sets alarm bells ringing. But the small companies Berkeley specialises in are not overborrowed like RJR Nabisco and other giants have been, it says, and allow more scope to step in and sort things out if the business gets into difficulties.

Berkeley's target is to be booking profits of $100m after tax (three times their 1989 level) in five year's time, and although the dollar profits give some currency risk the shares could be worth a punt at 199p. With profits expected to break $46m this year, giving a prospective PE ratio below 7, the shares are worth buying.

SOCK SHOP
Shop socks Sophie

With one of the worst tales of woe from the high street yet, Sock Shop announced last week that it expected to make a 'material' loss in the year to February. Analysts expect upcoming figures to show a loss of several millions of pounds in the six months to August, with losses for the year itself perhaps reaching £5m. In the wake of the news, the shares fell 20p to 45p, leaving Sock Shop valued at just £9.9m.

The shares, which came to the USM in 1987, reached 325p in 1988. A year ago, they stood at 162p after pre-tax profits for the 12 months to September 1988 jumped to £2.62m (£1.83m). In July, they slipped below 100p, as figures for the 17 months to February showed a fall in profits.

With hindsight, Sock Shop is being dismissed as a company that was hyped too much and expanded too fast, spending too much to open too many shops while the consumer boom was running out of steam. But, the most dramatic evidence that Sock Shop had overstretched came in the US, where it announced write-offs at the end of last year. This was accompanied by news of talks about a refinancing and restructuring. Some see this as the only hope for the company, but others wonder who might put up the cash. Anyone willing to bail Sock Shop out at the current share price 'needs their brains examined' was one less sanguine view.

Sugar daddy or not, there is little chance of investors seeing a profit. Chairman, Sophie Mirman and her husband Richard Ross still hold more than 80 per cent of the shares. Perhaps this is the only thing that has stopped the price falling further. **Sell.**

Investors Chronicle 9–15 February 1990

The *Investors Chronicle* is also concerned with precious metals, gilts and other fixed interest stocks, unit trusts and even returns on bank and building society accounts. The personal finance section features an 'Absolute Beginners' page. Do not be put off by its title, for as well as periodically explaining the basics about unit trusts, investment trusts and gilts, etc, it also covers such subjects as investment clubs, explains such matters as how the EMS works and unravels the mysteries of the ECU.

Financial Weekly

First published in 1979 as a newspaper, *Financial Weekly* has now switched to a magazine format. It is part of the Eurexpansion Network and is published each Friday at £1.40. The annual subscription is £47. Two and three-year subscriptions are offered at £80 and £110 respectively.

Financial Weekly does not address itself specifically to the private investor. It is a magazine for financial professionals in the City and in business. It is written for finance directors, chairmen and chief executives of major companies and for securities industry professionals. However, it is not without items of interest for the individual investor. Apart from giving the general background it also monitors the FTSE 100. The weekly table gives a range of statistics including share price changes over the previous week, quarter and year, together with pre-tax profit and earnings per share growth over one and five years. Its 'Analysts' Research section is a round-up of recommendations from leading investment analysts in UK stockbroking firms. The recommendations of buy, hold or sell are accompanied by a brief synopsis of the analysts' research.

Money Observer

Published by the *Observer* newspaper, *Money Observer* describes itself as the monthly magazine for discerning investors. It entered 1990 as the 'Personal Finance Magazine of the Year'. The current annual independent National Readership Survey has revealed that the publication has a readership of 250,000. Most certainly its in-house style is highly readable and it is also well presented. It is published at £2.25. The annual subscription is £24.50, or £20 if paid by direct debit.

Money Observer embraces the whole field of personal finance – everything from alternative investment (ie purchasing antiques, wine or collectables, etc with a view to a future capital gain) to unit and investment trusts and shares. In between, it covers such matters as endowment policies, accident insurance, pensions, tax, PEPs, bank and building society accounts.

It is a different animal from the *Investors Chronicle*, which, being a weekly, can offer 'instant reporting' of company results and report the 'very latest' financial news. However, *Money Observer* by no means ignores equities. Although with printing lead times any comment tends to be retrospective, its 'Throgmorton' column does contain tips. The magazine's 'Databank' provides a wealth of statistical information. Its 'Share Guide' gives the price performance of every UK listed share over one month, six months and one year.

The 'Unit Trust Databank' lists the top ten unit trusts in 20 sectors and also analyses every unit trust over monthly, quarterly, half-yearly and one, three and seven-year periods. The analysis is on the basis of £100 invested over the various periods. Each trust's overall ranking is also given. The performance of property bonds are given over one-, three- and seven-year periods. Index-Linked National Savings Certificates, popularly known as 'Granny Bonds' feature in a table which shows how a £100 investment has grown in value at monthly purchase dates from June 1975. Finally, the top ten performing investment trusts are given in 18 sectors. The performance of every trust is given over one-, three- and seven-year periods.

Moneywise

Moneywise describes itself as 'The Magazine it Pays You to Buy'. It is the newest personal finance magazine on the market; issue one appeared in June, 1990. However, despite its newness it does have an excellent pedigree. It originates from the merger of *Money Magazine* and *Family Wealth Magazine*, which later became *Money*. Early in 1990 the title was acquired by Berkeley Magazines Limited, a subsidiary of The Reader's Digest Association Limited. It is published monthly at £1.75 per issue.

Moneywise is an all-embracing publication. It is about investing and planning for the future, but it also covers earning, spending, borrowing and buying. The magazine is aimed at homeowners who want to protect the value of their property and assets; savers who want to know how best to invest their income; parents who want to provide for their own and their children's future; shoppers who want value for the money they spend; and families who want independent, down-to-earth advice on the financial issues that touch their lives.

The Private Investor

An upmarket glossy quarterly published by Telecoms Publications at £2.50. Do not expect share tips here, but, if you are looking for well-informed general features written by top financial journalists, look no further.

Although written with the businessman in mind, the private investor will also find it of interest. Contributors are generally editors or specialist correspondents from other publications. Equities, unit and investment trusts, PEPs and insurance policies are covered, but retrospectively rather than with a view to the future.

Money Management

Money Management is a *Financial Times* publication written for professional advisers. Individual copies cost £2.85 and the annual subscription is £49.50 by first-class post and £42 by second-class mail. As one would expect with anything from the FT stable, standards are high.

Although aimed at the professional, there is nothing to stop the private investor taking a peep at what the professionals are reading. Indeed, it is a way of ascertaining if your own adviser is well enough informed! The 'Market Briefing' and 'Product News' sections keep readers abreast of development. There are general features and a host of statistical information on unit trusts, exempt funds, insurance funds and details of building society rates, etc.

The publication does not embrace specific shares, but is more orientated towards 'financial products'. Although one of the professionals' 'bibles', it is not without interest to individuals, particularly those who are devotees to unit trusts and financial products generally.

Conclusion

There is a wealth of financial information available. It is impossible to read it all and it is certainly not worth subscribing to everything. A publication which appeals to one individual may well be considered unacceptable by another. Everyone must decide which publications fulfil their own needs. Ask stockbrokers if they will forward their newsletters and browse through what is on offer at larger newsagents. Only subscribe to a magazine once you have decided that meets your requirements and the style appeals. Do look out for special subscription offers.

If you have a group of friends who are interested in the investment scene, there is always the possibility of pooling resources and sharing the cost of subscriptions. Theoretically, this should work well, but, if everyone is to benefit from the material, there must be strict guidelines as to the length of time each individual retains a specific periodical. In other words, the smaller the group of individuals in an informal 'financial library', the better. Remember that marketmakers also read the financial press and it may well be prudent to act later rather than immediately if a particular share is tipped.

There is always the possibility, of course, that your local library subscribes to financial publications. If this is the case, a personal subscription may not be necessary. Should copies of a particular magazine not be stocked, do bear in mind that the committee which decides which magazines to take is far more likely to submit to popular demand. Written suggestions for subscriptions for specific periodicals can work wonders.

5
Look and Listen

'*TV just feeds you. Radio involves you*' Himan Brown, 1974

Television and radio

Considering that there are now four television channels in the UK, it is surprising that a good *regular* financial television spot has not yet appeared which can satisfy the needs of the average private sector.

One possible explanation as to why television should appear to be out of touch with what the public wants, is that there is no regular peak viewing slot for financial matters. Admittedly there are the *Money Programme* (on BBC 2) and the *City Programme* (ITV). The former presently appears at 1835 hours on Sundays, the latter at 2235 hours on Thursdays. To cram everything the Editors would like to cover into a 30–40 minute slot is impossible. And, as the frequency of both programmes is weekly, one has either to make the decision to exclude all the current news (including it in the *Money Programme* on a Sunday evening means it would be stale), or to restrict the coverage to general newsworthy topics and that news which is current. The *City Programme* has the timing advantage.

When BBC 2 launched the *Money Programme*, it was aimed more towards those with an active general interest in finance, but now it covers finance generally and not necessarily items to interest the investing public. The result is that the *Money Programme* offers good background information with in-depth coverage of certain events, but generally excludes up-to-the-minute news coverage. Certainly the programme is worth viewing and its content is always varied.

The *City Programme*, as its name implies, is concerned with the Square Mile and its activities. The programme is lively and its producer is to be congratulated at the amount of diverse material that is covered in less than half an hour. Undoubtedly, it will appeal to those with an interest in the stock market. Its Cityfile,

CityLine and City View slots are particularly good. The programme includes the views of a wide cross-section of analysts, company chairmen and city figures. Its main drawback is that it is not broadcast more frequently than weekly.

Admittedly, Channel 4 screens *Business Daily* each Monday to Friday, excluding Public Holidays, at 1230 hours. This programme offer up-to-the-minute news. Its prime target is City people, but only those with television sets in their offices who have the time to sit back for half an hour each day to see what is going on around them. In other words, it is mainly for the gratification of those in the 'City Club'. However, you can record the programme and watch it at your leisure in the evening.

Financial news does feature on the main TV news programmes throughout the day. However, it is only the main highlights that appear and even those are only in terms that will appeal to a mass audience. This is one of the problems. Those interested in the stock market are small in proportion to the total TV audience. Today, the name of the game is audience numbers. If a subject does not have mass appeal, then unfortunately the air time that will be allocated to it is small and then likely to be at non-peak viewing hours.

There is certainly a need for a good personal finance programme on television. This should embrace the whole of the financial scene and not be restricted just to investments. At a conference entitled *Managing Personal Sector Debt* held in March 1990, Marie Jennings, Deputy Chairman of the Money Management Council, claimed that consumers were increasingly becoming prey to easy credit and sophisticated sales techniques. Delegates to the conference also heard that despite millions having been spent by the Government and the finance industry on investor protection there has still been a failure to educate the consumer on financial matters. Education is the finest form of protection that the public can have and a good, lively personality finance programme on TV would go a long way to protecting consumers from loan sharks and those offering dubious investment opportunities.

A 15-minute television programme each evening showing the latest City news would also be welcomed by many. It could give company results, have a brief market report and feature the main news of the day such as bids and deals, and give brief details of any company making its debut in the market in the future. Clearly there would have to be safeguards against hyping shares, unit trusts or particular investment products.

Radio, on the other hand, adequately caters for those interested in financial matters. For real enthusiasts living in the London area, the first financial broadcast of the day is on LBC from 0500 to 0600 hours. Called *Dawn Traders* it is aimed at dealers and the like heading towards their desks in the City of London. It is a programme aimed at professionals and its standards are high. There is a resumé of developments on the world's stock markets which were closing while London slept. Much of the content will not be of interest to small investors and it is unlikely that the hour will appeal! Nevertheless, it gives an interesting insight into the information that is important to those at the hub in the City. LBC also broadcasts a share check at half past every hour between 0930 hours and 1630 hours, Monday to Friday. The service was discontinued for a brief period, but had to be restored because of popular demands. LBC, in common with other local radio stations throughout the country, also has programmes and phone-ins on personal finance.

An excellent personal finance programme is *Money Box*, which is broadcast on BBC Radio 4 at noon on Saturday. There is a repeat at 1000 hours on Mondays. Do not except tips on shares, a market report, or share prices, but it is a good all-round programme which embraces all aspects of personal finance from credit to savings, insurance plans to unit trusts. Radio 4 also caters for those interested in the City. At 2145 hours Monday to Friday, *Financial World Tonight* is broadcast. This 15-minute slot covers the markets, company news such as results, bids and deals, as well as the economic indicators. It also contains some excellent interviews with analysts, company chairmen and leading City figures.

There are two other good financial spots on Radio 4. At 0645 hours Monday to Friday, there is *Business News* which is part of the *Today* programme. It includes a brief report of the previous day's events, what has happened overnight on other markets and outlines the events which will occur during the day, eg companies which will be reporting, deadlines for bid offers, and economic figures which will be reported in the *Six O'clock News*. The *Six O'clock News* includes a market report and highlights of the day's main financial news.

However, 'looking and listening' is not only restricted to TV and radio programmes as will now be revealed.

Teletext

If you have a television with access to Teletext, you will be able to bring the very latest financial news on to your own TV screen. Simply select the BBC 2 channel, switch to the Teletext mode and Ceefax is at your fingertips. The City news begins on page 200. Select Channel 4 and Oracle's financial news and features are there for your perusal. Its City news begins on page 500. Both Ceefax and Oracle offer a similar service, the deciding factor as to which to use falls on personal preference. With this in mind we will now take a look at what Ceefax offers.

As with newspapers, the services begin with headlines. The headlines page also gives the FT-SE Index, Wall Street's Dow Jones Index, Tokyo's Nikkei Index, the price of gold and oil and the US$:£ exchange rate. The numbers relate to the pages which contain the new stories. For example, on 3 March 1990, Ceefax's page 203 read:

O'REILLY UNVEILS WATERFORD RESCUE
Heinz chairman Mr Tony O'Reilly has launched his eagerly awaited rescue of debt-ridden Waterford Wedgwood.

His Dublin-based investment vehicle, Fitzwilton has teamed up with bankers Morgan Stanley to subscribe I£79m (at 37½p) for an effective 29.9% stake in the troubled glass-to-china combine.

At the same time, Waterford itself is raising a further I£22.8m by way of a one-for-five rights issue at just 27½p.

The combined proceeds which should add up to a net of I£96.3m will go to reduce the group's considerable borrowings.

At the bottom of each page, the viewer is directed to four other services within the City Section. Each has a different colour. The 'colour code' is always in the same order: red, green, yellow and blue. They are known as 'prompts'. These may read, Next News, Citywatch, Headlines and Cityflash. The colour keys on the remote control correspond to the Ceefax pages in the colour the prompt is written in. In our example, pressing the red key will result in the text relating to the next headline appearing, ie the details of the UK official reserves increasing. Please note that although the index may not appear in page order, the actual pages do follow numerical convention.

Cityflash is simply what its name implies. A page number will be given for further details. Thus, a 'flash' relating to the FT-SE 100 close will point the viewer towards the Market's page. This will give details of the FT-SE close for each day of the last and current account in bar chart form as well as details of the index's progress during the day. The same information is given for the FT-30 Index (the page also gives the FT-All Share and Gilts Index), while another page gives the same treatment to the Dow Jones Index. The World Indices page gives the following indices:

Amsterdam	(EDE)
Australia	(AD)
Frankfurt	(DAX)
Hong Kong	(HS)
Paris	(CAC)
Singapore	(STI)
Tokyo	(NDJ)
Zurich	(SPI)

Ceefax does not just report market statistics, like a newspaper, it also has its stock market report. This is how it read on 3 March 1990:

The London stock market ended the week on a bright note.

Sentiment was cheered by gains in Tokyo and New York and advice from brokers Warburgs recommending selective buying in the coming months.

However, sterling's continued losses kept investors in a cautious mood.

Turnover was swollen by the placing of Elders 23% stake in Scottish and Newcastle (down 9p to 310p).

The weaker pound depressed gilts, which shed up to three-quarters of a point.

On the bid front, Sketchley slumped 98p to 251p as Godfrey Davis withdrew its bid in the wake of Sketchley's profits warning on Thursday.

Chemoxy, though, gained 48p to 450p, as agreed bid terms from Suter bettered an unwelcome advance from MTM.

Among leaders, Thorn EMI was relieved that an offer Griffen records was unlikely, but GrandMet (13p lower at 547p) suffered from adverse comment.

This particular report ran to two pages. The pages 'turn' automatically. Although there is normally adequate time to read the screen, if for any reason a slower pace is required, the pages can be put on 'hold' via the remote control. Briefer market reports are also given for Wall Street, the Far East (Australia, Hong Kong, Singapore and Tokyo).

The service's European market report currently only covers Frankfurt and Amsterdam. Not surprisingly in a comprehensive service, there is a foreign exchange report. A range of exchange rates is also given for a variety of currencies. The rates are given for trade deals as well as for tourists. UK and US interest rates are given in addition to savings rates, which will be of most interest to the private investor. These are the rates that were listed on Ceefax at 5 March 1990:

Short
Money Fund Account (call)
3 year Gilt
Building Society (call)
Bank Deposit (7 days)

Medium
National Investment Account (1 month)
National Savings Income Bond (3 months)

Long
National Savings Certificate* (8 months)
National Savings Capital Bond (3 months)
5 year Government Investment Bond

a 5 year investment term

Interest rates are given for nil, 25 per cent and 40 per cent tax bands. The withdrawal notice is given in brackets.

The Ceefax Unit Trust Panel's monthly selection will be of interest to the small investor. Extracts from the selection for March 1990 are given below as an example of what to expect, but note that the information is historic.

The **CEEFAX Unit Trust Panel** has been recruited from a number of independent advisory firms in an attempt to offer a path through the unit trust jungle.

Unit trusts, it must be emphasised, can fall in value. Neither the panellists nor the BBC can accept responsibility for recommendations made.

Selections shown and opinions expressed are those of the persons named and are not necessarily shared by the BBC.

*Investors are recommended always to seek professional advice before buying.

MARCH selections:

	UK	USA	Japan	Gilts	Other
Kelvin Borhani					*
Mark Dampier	*		*		*
Peter Edwards	*		*		*

*Selections are geared for growth on a 12-month view and are considered worthy of inclusion in a balanced portfolio. S indicates a speculative investment.

Kelvin Borhani (Murray Noble)
*March commentary
Overview: Interest rates worldwide seem to be on an upward trend once again.

Japan needs to support the yen, Germany has to combat inflation, America needs to finance its budget deficit and the rest of the world has little choice but to follow suit.

No respite for businesses, properties, or countries in the Third World. One cannot help feeling the whole financial system is tangled in a vicious circle and needs its own perestroika!
Japan: More fireworks expected. Avoid.
UK: High inflation, high trade deficit, lower profits, and high interest rates. Hold for now.
USA: Deficits show little sign of improving. Corporate results have been disappointing. Hold for now.
Europe: Still promises to be a growth area. Buy either Henderson European or Fidelity European.

Mark Dampier: (Whitechurch Securities)
*March commentary
Overview: Markets have again proved volatile. Investors need to keep a cool nerve and buy on gloomy days. The doom merchants normally overplay their hand.

Inflation fears are overdone worldwide and the recent hike in interest rates should provide a buying opportunity for international bonds. Both cashflow and liquidity remain strong and this should provide the basis for a strong rally some time this year. In thin markets a move-up could come very quickly on a change in sentiment.
UK: Buy GT Smaller Companies Dividend and the new Newton General Trust.
Japan/Far East: Stick to a general fund such as the new Schroder Far Eastern Growth.
Europe. Stick to quality. Try Abtrust European.
USA: Avoid for the time being.

Peters Edwards: (Premier UT Brokers)
*March commentary

General: Cheer Up! 1990 will improve. Last month's turbulence has provided bargains everywhere. So take advantage.

Concentrate overseas for now, with at least half your portfolio in America, Europe and Japan. The next run on the pound will more than recover your costs.

Later in the year get set to repatriate profits, London shares will blast off when cash-rich institutions sniff lower interest rates.

UK: Hold proven income funds such as Capability Income and Growth, Framlington Extra Income, but don't expect progress yet. Leave Smaller Company funds.

Europe: Current market prices are more realistic after New Year euphoria. Use a good general fund like Mercury European, not a single market fund.

Japan: When the authorities stop squabbling about how to stem inflation, the yen will stabilise. Funds such as Schroder Tokyo will then motor again.

Followers of shares will be pleased to learn that Ceefax devotes pages to company results. The coverage is brief, but adequate. After giving the company name and its line of business, the following data is given:

> Dividend – Final or Interim
> Pre-tax Profits (or loss)
> Earnings or Loss per Share
> *Property profit
> *Extraordinary Credit Turnover
> +Pre-Tax Revenue
> +Net Asset Value
> *where appropriate
> +for investment trusts

After the data, two or three lines may be added which those who compile Ceefax consider relevant. It may be the Chairman's comments or news of an acquisition.

Ceefax is extremely useful for checking share and gilt prices, but do not expect the 'Share Prices' page of the *Financial Times* to appear on your screen. The *Sharecheck* service only covers shares with a full listing and is restricted to ten pages. Nevertheless, it does currently list 150 shares. The pages are grouped into 'sets' of three or four. Each group of pages automatically turns. For example, shares listed alphabetically AAH–HAN may appear on four pages, shares HAR–RAT on three pages, etc. By keying 221, the four pages with shares listed alphabetically AAH–HAN will sequentially appear; keying 222 will bring three pages of shares listed alphabetically HAR–RAT sequentially on to the screen. The prices are updated on business days at 0915, 1045, 1215, 1345, 1515 and 1730 hours. However, please note that Ceefax financial services close at noon on a Saturday. *Sharecheck* gives no data other than the price and the movement since the previous close. For High–Low, PE and yield data, you must refer to a quality newspaper.

The prices of 30 USM shares are listed on a single page. Another page is devoted to the prices of 30 recent issues. New issues are added and others deleted on a weekly basis. The gilts page lists 14 British funds. There are other features of the prices service. 'Movers' is devoted the biggest gainers and losers. Prices are also given for commodities. For example, the following information is given at the close:

Bullion
London

Gold:	Previous day's opening and close today's price and today's close.
Silver, Spot and 3 month:	Previous day's fix and close and today's fix and close.
Coins:	Britannia, Krugerrand, New Sovereign and Platinum Noble. Prices for previous day's close, am and closing prices.

New York

Gold:	Current and next month. Previous day's close, today's opening and close.
Silver:	Current and two months later. Previous day's close, today's opening and close.

Base Metals
London Metal Exchange

Copper Lead Tin	Cash: previous day and today's close.
Zinc Sheeting Aluminium Nickel	3 months: close two days ago and current close.

New York Coinex

Copper (two months later)	Previous day's close, today's opening and close – settlement prices.

Prices are also given for 'softs' (eg cocoa, coffee, sugar, etc) and farm prices.

Investors on the lookout for new issues will possibly find the 'Coming to the Market' page of interest. However, it gives only a small proportion of the information contained in the 'New Issue' page of the *Investors Chronicle*.

Ceefax offers a reasonable service given its constraints of space. At times, the service is infuriatingly slow, but no doubt technology will solve this minor irritation at some future date.

Oracle, on the other hand, is a faster service. Its main content is much in line with Ceefax's. However, its personal finance pages are far superior. In addition to news, features and information on mortgages, taxation and National Savings, there is even a letters page, just like a newspaper. Indeed Oracle even includes advertisements. The main difference between the services is in their presentation. There is no charge for using Teletext, so both services can be used without creating additional expenditure. Discerning viewers should select the best features from each.

Information by telephone

When Teleshare was launched in May 1987, the *USM Magazine* described it as 'the most important development for the private investor since the Stock Exchange emerged from the coffee shop'. Praise indeed. The birth of the telephone publishing industry in the UK was a result of the Government liberalising telecommunications.

The industry has experienced dynamic growth with an annual turnover of £23m in 1986, rising to above £160m in 1989. It is expected that turnover will exceed £250m in 1992. A range of services is provided by the telephone information companies. They extend from weather reports to real-time financial information from the London Stock Exchange.

The launch of telephone financial services was revolutionary. For the first time ever investors could obtain the very latest share prices in their home, at the office, from a pay telephone or from a hotel room when they wished. The service also offers the latest FT-SE 100 Index, market reports and a host of other information. The four main companies offering a telephone financial service are:

- Citycall on 071-247 1557;
- FT Cityline on 071-925 2128;
- Sharecall on 071-242 1002; and
- Teleshare on 071-975 9000.

Perhaps the most progressive of the companies is Telephone Information Services Limited which provides Teleshare. This was the first interactive real-time share price service in the UK. Membership is free and members automatically receive an Index and User Guide listing around 4000 shares and securities as well as a portfolio facility and membership card. You do not have to be a member to take advantage of the service. However, you will require a modern push-button multi-frequency (MF) tone telephone. If you are not sure whether your own telephone is suitable, and to hear a demonstration of the service, simply telephone 0895 500 590 and follow the simple test instructions. Teleshare can provide an MF model for £25 inclusive of VAT, postage and packing. Alternatively, a tone generator, which is suitable for converting most telephones, is available at £10 inclusive of VAT, postage and packing. This can be handy for investors who travel. Teleshare can be contacted at:

Telephone Information Services Limited
24 West Smithfield
London EC1A 9DL

Teleshare gives access to around 400 real–time share prices, which is more than those listed on the *Financial Times'* 'London Share Service' pages. All Alpha, Beta and Gamma shares are featured in the Teleshare service, which includes most of the USM and Third Market shares, all Gilts, Rights Issues and all foreign stocks quoted on the London Stock Exchange. The prices are accessed from SEAQ and SEAQ International.

In addition, an increasing range of financial bulletins is a significant component of the Teleshare service. These include:

- exchange rates for sterling against major trading currencies;
- exchange rates for the US dollar against major trading currencies;
- tourist rates of exchange for major holiday destinations;
- company results;
- company news;
- bullion prices and news;
- oil prices and news;

- fast moving shares (active shares of the day);
- a stock market summary (updated eight times a day with a review of the previous hour plus sector reports and news);
- FT-SE 100 Index in 'real-time';
- ISE/AMEX/XMI Index (SEAQ International);
- ISE/NIKKEI 50 (SEAQ International);
- FT30/FT500/FT All Share/£/Trade Weighted Index;
- overseas reports;
- Wall Street reports;
- Forexia currency analysis for sterling/deutschmark/Japanese yen and US dollar;
- City preview (a diary of forthcoming events and announcements);
- market review (a round-up of the previous week's events).

The Teleshare Index also gives the four digit numbers for the full range of its bulletins and other services. For example, one facility is to obtain bid and offer prices for all shares. Perhaps the most useful service for the private investor is the opportunity to key in an individual number. By following simple instructions investors can create their own 'portfolio' and add or delete holdings at any time. It works like this. Members access Teleshare and key in a given four-digit number. They can then key in the Teleshare Index number for up to 20 shares. When you want to know how the shares in your portfolio are performing, you follow simple instructions and will immediately be told the price of the shares in your portfolio. There are simple instructions for adding or deleting shares to the portfolio. No additional charge is made for this service.

As previously mentioned, there is no joining or annual membership fee. However, the service is not without charge. In common with all '0898' numbers, use of the service costs 38 pence per minute at peak times, or 25 pence per minute during off-peak periods, ie after 1800 hours but before 0800 hours at weekdays or at any time during weekends or public holidays. Parts of a minute are charged at 5 pence per 8 and 12 seconds for peak and off-peak use respectively. The following newspapers are currently linked to Teleshare:

- *Daily Telegraph*;*
- *Daily Mirror*;
- *Daily Express*;
- *Eastern Daily Press*,* Eastern Counties Newspapers

- *Evening Echo** Essex
- *Liverpool Daily Post**
- *Manchester Evening News**
- *Northern Echo**
- *Portsmouth Echo**

*Full 'own branded' Teleshare service

The *Daily Telegraph* launched its Teleshare service in December 1987. It is exactly the same as the standard Teleshare service. The four-digit Index Numbers for specific shares are published in Monday editions of the newspaper on its 'Share Prices' page, alongside the names of the stock. As with the Teleshare service, membership is free and tone generators or MF telephones are available at £10 and £25 respectively. Although one does not have to join Teleshare to take advantage of the service (provided one has access to the four-digit Index Numbers), it makes sound sense to take advantage of the free membership. Members receive:

- an Index Directory which incorporates a user guide;
- a membership card which incorporates a personal portfolio number and abbreviated user guide;
- a letter of welcome and introduction;
- twice yearly newsletters.

As a rough indication of the costs of accessing share prices in a personal portfolio Teleshare estimates that the time taken to be given four prices is 30 seconds. Off-peak this works out at 12.5 pence. Prices are inclusive of VAT. Provided Teleshare is used sensibly, the costs can be modest. Telephone addicts would find their telephone bills mounting should they not be able to control their urges to check the state of their finances. However, as with all things, if used in moderation, all should be well.

6
Issues – New, Scrip and Rights

'You pays your money and you takes your choice' Punch, 1846

Introduction

The day of Britain's first mega company flotation was 3 December 1984, a day to be remembered in the history of the Stock Exchange. It was also the day that many took their first plunge in buying shares. Individuals who had previously been quite content with building society share accounts, bank deposits, National Savings Certificates and possibly dipping their toes into unit trusts, discovered the wonders of direct investment in the Stock Exchange. However, even those who had not dabbled with unit trusts are in fact already likely to be shareholders by a roundabout route. Those who contribute to pension funds, or who pay endowment policy premiums are unwittingly indirectly investing in the stock market, for all pension fund managers and insurance companies have been channelling money into stocks and shares for years. It is no secret, but only those who take the trouble of ascertaining where their hard-earned money goes know that they are indirectly investing in companies at home and overseas. But what was the event that stirred the imaginations of so many?

It was the privatisation of British Telecom (BT). It was not the first occasion that the Government had sold shares of a state-owned company, but it was the first time that it had really wooed the public with a view to wider share ownership. Commercials appeared on TV and advertisements were published in the press to whet the appetite. The prospectus and application forms were duly published. The PR machinery had worked well. In the event over two million private individuals took up the Government's BT privatisation offer. It was considerably oversubscribed and, in the event, no individual received more than 800 shares. Offered at £1.35 with 50p to be paid on application, the partly paid shares closed on the first day of trading at 95p. In other words, £400 was transformed into £760, less of course, broker's commission, etc. Those who were not tempted to cash in their holdings saw their investment triple after two months.

Of course, not all new issues have been so successful. It must always be emphasised that the value of shares and the income from them can go down as well as up. Also, while the past performance of the stock market has been good in the long term, it must always be remembered that past performance is not necessarily an indication of the future. Above all, bear in mind that shares must generally be viewed as a medium- to long-term investment. In other words, it is not a suitable home for funds that you may need in a hurry. Keep a nest egg in a form of investment that does not fluctuate in value, eg a building society or bank account, for emergencies. Until you have a financial cushion, do not contemplate investing on the stock market.

Having given the caveats, it is now time to look at new issues, and once you are a shareholder, other situations that you may encounter.

New issues

There are various ways in which new issues can come to the market. In this section we will not distinguish between a full stock market listing, or companies that are offered on the Unlisted Securities Market (USM). However, it should be mentioned that the purchase of shares in a Government privatisation issue and buying shares in a new USM company are poles apart. Admittedly, many successful companies, such as Body Shop, have come into the market via the USM route, but generally it is a more volatile market than shares in companies with a full Stock Exchange listing. With exceptions acknowledged, the USM is not an investment ground for widows and orphans. Although the potential gains may be high, so are the risks. The three main ways in which a company may offer its shares to the market will now be outlined.

Placings

The new shares, or blocks of existing shares, are sold at a fixed price to institutions as well as to private investors. There is a lead broker and a co-sponsor broker and rules state the proportion of the issue that each may handle. This is to ensure a wider spread of ownership. It is not unusual for placings to result in hectic trading on their first day.

Offer by prospectus
The issue of shares direct to the public at a stated price or by tender (see *Offer for sale* below).

Offer for sale
This is similar to *Offer by prospectus*, but the shares being sold are first acquired by an issuing house or broker and then offered to the public.

Introduction
This is a method whereby an unquoted company with a fair spread of shareholders obtains a market listing on the Stock Exchange. There is no specific offer of securities, but the shareholders may agree to dispose of part of their holdings at an agreed price.

Sales by tender
This method was popular in the early to mid-1980s, but has since fallen from favour. However, as with fashions generally, even the method of being launched on the stock market has its popular forms. Perhaps sales by tender will become fashionable again.

Basically, it is nothing more than an auction with a reserve price. A company's shares are offered, say at a minimum of 200p each. Investors are invited to subscribe at this or a higher price. Normally, after all the 'bids' have been examined, a price is generally struck at which all the shares will be sold. If this is 220p, all those who tendered at this or a higher price will be allocated shares. Those who bid above 220p, will have the difference between the price at which they tendered and the striking price refunded. Every attempt is made to strike a price which is both fair to those selling the shares and to investors.
(Note: In some cases, applications are accepted at the bid price, so read the terms of the offer carefully.)

Prospectus

Whichever method is used to launch a company on the Stock Exchange or the USM, a prospectus is essential. It is produced by the merchant bank or stockbrokers sponsoring the issue and is drawn up so that it satisfies the requirements of the Companies Acts and Stock Exchange's regulations. The objective of a prospectus is to give potential investors information in order that they may assess the merits, or otherwise, of purchasing the shares. The result is a very detailed document which outlines the nature and development of the business, gives information about its management team, a host of details about its past and present financial position and outlines the company's future prospects. Professional investors study a prospectus extremely thoroughly. Indeed, all investors should follow this route, though few do, preferring to rely instead on press comment or the advice of their broker. Assessing all the facts in a prospectus is very time-consuming.

Finding out about new issues

It is nearly impossible to escape from a Government privatisation issue. The British Gas 'Ask Sid' campaign will be remembered for many years. However, other debuts to the market are more discreet. Ceefax contains a section on forthcoming issues and the *Investors Chronicle* has a 'New Issues' page which includes advance notice of future offerings, as well as giving details of what will be offered in the forthcoming week. Although placings are covered in the *Financial Times* and generally in the City pages of the quality national newspapers, greater coverage is given to offers for sale. The larger the issue, the greater the amount of column inches that will be devoted to the flotation.

It is difficult for private investors to obtain shares in a company through a placing. Applications for securities issued by a placing should be made through a broker in the usual way. The chances of becoming a 'founder' shareholder are greater if your own broker is involved in the issue. Offers for sale or shares offered by prospectus are the most accessible way to new share ownership by the general public.

For new USM issues you may have to apply to the sponsor direct for a prospectus – details will be given in the press notice(s) announcing the issue. With Stock Exchange flotations, the full prospectus and an application form are more likely to be printed in newspapers, but separate copies of the prospectus are still available from the sponsors. With Government privatisations, copies of the prospectus are also generally available from certain banks.

Deciding whether to buy

Ideally the prospectus should be read and your own conclusions reached. However, time may not permit such analysis. In any event, if the flotation is going to be successful, ie the shares open at a premium, what other investors think of the flotation is essential.

The alternative to doing your own research is to read what the financial journalists have to say about the matter. They will have done their rounds of the City and talked to institutions and stockbrokers. It would be prudent not to restrict yourself to the commentary of one newspaper, but to read two or three assessments of the flotation. Of course, there is no guarantee that anyone will be entirely right. Views can also change over time. When the privatisation of the water companies was announced, the City's reaction was initially lukewarm. However, as the flotation date approached, enthusiasm was generated. Although premiums of up to 40 per cent were mooted, no one anticipated that the demand would be so great. In this particular instance, the premium was underestimated.

Of course, the reverse situation can also occur. In fact, no one can accurately predict what will happen. Take the last sale of the Government's British Petroleum (BP) shares in 1987. The price was fixed by the experts at 330p. The initial payment was 120p with two calls of 105p in August 1988 and April 1989. All looked well at the time the price was announced. However, the offer opened on 20 October 1987, the day after Black Monday when the world's stock markets plummeted. All the careful calculations of the price were thrown into disarray. Only a few investors took the plunge and the underwriters were left with most of the 2194 million shares offered. On the first day of dealing, the partly paid shares opened at 88p and closed at 85p – in other words, a loss of 35p per share. Needless to say, after the fall of the world's stock markets, no journalist recommended the new BP issue.

It is also important to decide whether you are going to purchase the shares to add to your portfolio, or simply as a short-term speculation. The latter is known as 'stagging' in stock market jargon. Remember, with Government privatisations, loyal shareholders may be rewarded. For example, loyal founder shareholders in BT received a one-for-ten bonus issue of shares after three years, while founder shareholders in water companies, provided they were customers, could choose between a loyalty bonus issue of shares at a later date or a reduced final call. Remember, it is a criminal offence to submit multiple applications for Government privatisation issues. One MP found himself in prison for doing this (albeit briefly, but his political career was ruined), and other private investors have also been prosecuted. Multiple applications in the private sector are also frowned upon and those dealing with the issue attempt to 'weed out' such multiples.

Applying for a new issue

Before completing the application form, thought must be given to the number of shares you want to apply for. If the issue is going to be oversubscribed (the press will indicate if this is likely), do not anticipate receiving all the shares for which you apply. Indeed, you may not receive any. For example, Pickwick Group, the record company, was oversubscribed 50 times and one specialist retailer even topped that. Incidentally, the record for an opening premium goes to Sock Shop. The shares were offered at 125p. Dealings started at 205p and peaked on the first day at 290p before closing at 257p.

No one knows, in the event of an oversubscription, how the shares will be allocated. Here are a few possibilities.

- Applications for a small number of shares, eg 100 or 200, will be met in full.
- Those applying for up to 1000 shares will have their applications placed in a ballot to receive 200 shares. All other applicants will receive 10 per cent of what they applied for, subject to a maximum of 1000 shares.
- All applications will be placed in a 'weighted' ballot, eg those who applied for 2000 to 3000 shares will have a greater chance of receiving 200 shares, compared to those who applied for up to 1000 shares receiving 100 shares in the ballot, etc.
- All applications are 'scaled down'. For example, those who apply for up to 1000 shares receive 100. Those who apply for up to 2000 shares receive 200, etc.

The possible combinations are endless. It is most frustrating to apply, say, for shares costing £5000, and to receive a holding worth 10 per cent or even less of the payment accompanying the application. If successful in a ballot, or if your application is scaled down, your cheque is cashed and you receive a cheque for the value of the shares for which you unsuccessfully applied. Remember that at the end of the day, you are not earning interest on the funds you forwarded, or worse, are paying interest (possibly even an arrangement fee as well) on the money you borrowed in order to stag the issue.

Before the offer opens, there will generally be comment in the press regarding application tactics. Husbands and wives are normally advised, if an oversubscription is anticipated, to make separate as opposed to joint applications. If both are successful, the holding can be amalgamated at a later date. If a massive oversubscription is expected, potential investors are generally advised not to submit an application for a large amount. The reason is simple. To send a cheque for a few thousand pounds and to be allocated shares to the value of £200–300, does not make economic sense, for interest will be lost on the funds accompanying the application.

The advice is normally to apply for a more modest amount in the hope of either being lucky in the ballot, or that the allocation is large enough to definitely secure some shares. Read the advice tendered, but remember that at the end of the day it is anyone's guess what will happen. At least Government privatisations with their tendency to favour the small investor are more predictable than private sector flotations. Also, because of the size of Government issues, investors generally secure a 'reasonable' holding. Owning a mere handful of shares can be more trouble than they are worth.

In situations where the prospectuses and application forms are published in the press, matters could not be easier. In other situations, the prospectus and application form will have to be obtained from the sponsor (the press notice or the 'New Issues' section of the *Investors Chronicle* will identify the sponsor). Read the accompanying instructions before completing the application. Ensure that the form is completed correctly. One common error is to apply, say, for 1000 shares and sending a cheque in payment for 500. Do not forget to sign the application as well as your cheque! If applying by post, allow at least two days for delivery and always use first-class mail.

On occasions, especially for those living in or close to London, or near a provincial collecting point for applications, it is tempting to leave matters until the last moment and to deliver the application personally. The advantage of this is that applicants can take note of the very latest press comment.

If a 'grey' (ie unofficial) market in the shares has developed, there will be a better indication of the possible premium. However, if the issue is likely to be extremely popular, do not expect to stroll into the office dealing with the issue and hand your application in before the deadline, which is normally 1000 hours on the day the offer closes.

On the day the offer for the water companies closed, a queue started to form at National Westminster Bank's New Issue Department near the Bank of England at around 0830 hours. By 0930 hours it stretched several hundred yards. Many potential investors were still hundreds of yards from the entrance to the building when its doors were ceremoniously slammed shut (some would say unceremoniously) at 1000 hours precisely. At least a thousand would-be investors had lost their chance. In the event of an issue being fully subscribed, late applications are not accepted.

Monitoring the outcome of issues

Considering the volume of applications dealt with, the institutions generally work extremely efficiently. There have been hiccups, the largest bungle in recent years being the handling of the Abbey National flotation. However, thankfully, mishaps are not common. The prospectus will indicate when allotment letters (ie the official notification that the applicant has been allotted a specific number of shares) will be posted to those who have been successful. In the event of a massive oversubscription, however, it may not always be possible to adhere to such a timetable.

After the offer has closed, the press, TV and radio will report developments. If there has been an oversubscription, this will be announced and by how much. It will also be reported when the sponsors are going to reveal the basis of the allocation. Naturally, the allocation itself will also be reported. Likewise, if there is to be a delay in forwarding the allotment letters, this will be announced. It can be an anxious time for applicants. If there is a ballot, will an individual be successful? Or has the application arrived on time? All will be revealed in due course. However, those who cannot wait can enquire at their bank to ask if their cheque has been cashed. Provided the sponsors have only banked those of the successful applicants and not all cheques, it is possible to ascertain whether all is well.

The prospectus will announce when dealing will begin. As the date approaches, the press will report more accurate predictions of the likely premium. From the first day of dealing, the press will report prices for new issues.

Selling new issues

It is not prudent to sell a new issue until the allotment letter has been received or you definitely know that you have been successful. Brokers will normally want sight of the allotment letter when new shares are being sold by non-customers.

The 'Guidance Notes' notes on an allotment letter (which effectively is an interim share certificate) will instruct shareholders what to do with the document in the event of selling all or part of the shares it represents. The following is typical.

> *If you want to sell some or all of your shares*
> You can do this by instructing a bank or stockbroker to sell your shares on the Stock Exchange. Complete Form A overleaf having carefully read the instructions. Send or deliver the whole document to your bank or stockbroker.

The instructions are clear and the necessary action simple. All that is required is to complete the relevant boxes with the number of shares you are selling (one box in words, another in figures) and the box indicating the shares to be retained if the entire holding is not being sold. (In this event an allotment letter will be issued for the balance.) The signature(s) of the seller(s) will then be required. Letters in joint names should be signed by all parties.

Rights issues

Introduction

Occasions can arise in a company's development when it requires funds to expand its business further, for a specific venture, or to strengthen the company's finances generally. Money may be raised by way of a loan. Provided the cost of the indebtedness does not exceed the profits generated by using the money borrowed, this method of financing should be beneficial for shareholders. However, a company may decide that it does not want to borrow more money, for its indebtedness may already be at a prudent level. An alternative is to raise money from existing shareholders. This is known as a 'rights issue'.

One of the attractions of new equity capital to a company is that, unlike the cost of borrowing, there is no fixed cost. Borrowing money means that interest will have to be paid, whether or not the company is profitable. With share capital it is different. Investors are rewarded by sharing the company's profits. If the profits are not increased, the dividend may not necessarily rise. As explained below, if the prospects for a company are good, a rights issue can be very beneficial for investors.

Deciding whether to take up your rights

Naturally the first consideration should be your own financial position. Only you can decide whether you can afford the investment. Whatever the state of your finances, action must be taken before the offer closes. Even if financial resources are not a problem, it has to be decided whether to take advantage of the issue or whether to sell all or part of your rights. The latter is dealt with below. (Note: If you cannot afford all your rights issue entitlement, part of it can be sold and part taken up.)

The factors that will determine your action are the state of the company's finances, its prospects and the reason why the capital is required. The amount of capital being raised will also be a consideration as will the terms of the offer. If the company's prospects are favourable, then the market will react positively to the announcement. The reverse may be the case if the capital is required to support an ailing concern. The press will comment on the virtues or otherwise of individual rights issues.

Technical aspects

When shares are issued at a discount, it might be considered that something is being obtained for nothing. Rest assured, just as there is no such thing as a free lunch, free shares are also a figment of the imagination. An example will illustrate the point.

Suppose that an imaginary company, Issue Right Limited, wishes to raise more capital from its shareholders. Assume that the following are the background facts:

Number of shares currently issued	4 million
Current market price	200p

Suppose that Issue Right wanted to raise £2 million. There are many different combinations of the number of new shares issued and issue prices that will result in the desired objective. For example, here are a few possibilities:

- issue 1,000,000 shares at 200p;

- issue 1,250,000 shares at 160p;
- issue 2,500,000 shares at 80p.

It is most unlikely that the directors of Issue Right Limited would feel easy at deciding on an issue price of 200p. They would want a safety net against the current market price weakening on the announcement, or indeed against a general market fall. It will therefore want to offer the shares at a discount.

However, regardless of the price at which the company issues the new shares and provided all other factors remain unaltered, the value of an investor's holding after a rights issue has been taken up will equal the value of the shares before the issue, added to the cash sum paid to secure the new shares. The reason is simple. If new shares are offered at a discount, the price of the company's shares after going 'ex-rights' is proportional to the amount at which the new shares were issued.

An example will illustrate the point. Suppose Issue Right Limited calculated the theoretical ex-rights price of issuing shares at 200p, 160p and 80p. The 'terms of the offer' are self-explanatory. At 200p, a million new shares will have to be offered to raise £2m, the new shares will be offered to existing shareholders on the basis of one new share for every four old ones held – in stockmarket jargon this is a '1-for-4 issue'. At 160p, the term of the offer would be a 5-to-16 issue as 1.25 million shares would be needed to raise £2 million (the ratio 1.25m:4m is the same as 5:16), etc. The calculation of the theoretical ex-rights price is shown in Table 6.1.

Let us now suppose that a shareholder in Issue Right Limited has 400 shares at the time the rights issue is announced. By comparing the value of these at the day the new issue is announced against the value of his holding at the theoretical ex-rights price, it can be shown that for each of three prices used in our previous example the shareholder will be no better off it it is assumed: (1) that the rights are taken up; and (2) other factors remain unaltered.

As Table 6.2 illustrates, regardless of the discount, theoretically the investor is no better off.

It is tempting to ask why investors should bother taking up a rights issue if they will be no better off. It must be remembered that the examples are pure theory. If a company is well run and prosperous, it will put the capital to good use and increase the total value of the business. This will, other things being equal,

Table 6.1 *Issue Rights Ltd rights issue possibilities explored*

Market price before issue	Terms of issue	Price of new shares	Calculation of ex-rights price	Theoretical ex-rights price[1]
200p	1 for 4	200p	$$\dfrac{(4 \times 200\text{p}) + (1 \times 200\text{p})}{5}$$	200p
200p	5 for 16	160p	$$\dfrac{(16 \times 200\text{p}) + (5 \times 160\text{p})}{21}$$	190.5p
200p	5 for 8	80p	$$\dfrac{(8 \times 200\text{p}) + (5 \times 80\text{p})}{13}$$	153.8

[1]Shares are only traded in whole or half pence. However, this has been ignored when calculating the theoretical ex-rights price. Prices have been rounded up.

Note: The calculations assume that all other factors which affect price remain unaltered.

Table 6.2 *The effect of a rights issue in Issue Right Ltd*

Holding	Market price before issue p	Value of holding before issue £	Terms of issue	New share entitlement	Total price paid £	New share holding	Theoretical ex-rights price[1] p	Value of holding after issue[2] £
400	200	800	1 for 4 @ 200p	100	200	500	200.0	1000
400	200	800	5 for 16 @ 160p	125	200	525	190.5	1000
400	200	800	5 for 8 @ 80p	250	200	650	153.8	1000

[1] See Table 6.1
[2] The 'rounding' factor from Table 6.1 has been ignored.

benefit the shareholder in two ways. First there will be an increase in the share price. It may not be immediate, unless of course the market takes the potential increased prosperity into account. As was outlined in Chapter 1, the price of a share is determined by supply and demand. If the shares are sought by those who wish to participate in the company's future success, then this will normally result in an upward movement in the share price.

Second, an increased profitability will result in larger dividends per share after even a heavily discounted rights issue. This will be an added bonus to those who took up the rights, as it effectively increased the distribution on the new holding. Taking up a rights issue also means that your percentage stake in the company remains the same as before, whereas if the rights are sold, your stake in the company will have been diluted. In-depth analysis in the press of the desirability or otherwise of a particular rights issue will examine all the influencing factors.

The mechanics of a rights issue

Those who are entitled to participate in a rights issue will be issued with a provisional allotment letter (allotment letter). When it is received it is important to check that the correct number of shares has been allotted. This is particularly so if an addition has recently been added to your holding. Contact your broker if anything is amiss.

All the necessary instructions regarding taking up the rights in full, selling part and taking up the remainder or selling all will be fully outlined in the allotment letter. There is no denying that at first sight it all looks very complex. Allotment letters must not be ignored, for, if you do nothing by the stated date, you will lose your entitlement to subscribe for the new shares and your allotment letter will be valueless. If you are in any doubt what to do consult your financial adviser.

If you want to take up all your rights, then simply send the allotment letter, together with your cheque for the total amount due, to the institution dealing with the matter. As timing is essential, allow at least two or three days for postal delays. After a few days, the allotment letter will be returned stamped 'paid'. Until a share certificate for your new holding is received, the allotment letter is proof of ownership of your new shares – in other words, it acts as provisional share certificate.

Selling rights

Other things being equal, a provisional allotment letter has value. In theory, each share it represents is worth the difference between the market price before issue less the theoretical ex-rights price, adjusted for the terms of the offer so as to give the value of the right to subscribe for one new share. The concept is best illustrated with an example. Take the example in Table 6.2 of a 5-for-16 rights in Issue Right Limited at 160p. The value of each right is as follows:

$$(200p - 190.5p) \times \frac{16}{5} = \underline{30.4p}$$

Should our fictitious shareholder decide to sell his rights the gross proceeds will be £38 (125 × 30.4p). When the shares have gone ex-rights the 'theoretical' value of the holding will be £762 (400 × 190.5p). In other words, the shareholder's financial position will be same as before the rights issue. However, instead of having shares worth £800, it will be in the form of shares and cash valued at £800 (£762 + £38).

The example in Table 6.1 of a 5-for-8 rights in Issue Right Limited at 80p would have the same end result. The value of each right in this case would be:

$$(200 - 153.8p) \times \frac{8}{5} = 73.9p$$

In theory, the position ex-rights would still be £800 if the rights were sold:

	£
Gross proceeds of sale of rights (250 × 73.9p)	184.75
Value of original shares at the theoretical ex-rights price (400 × 153.8 = £615.20)	615.25 (1)
	£800.00

(1) Adjusted for 5p rounding factor

Of course, theory does not always go hand-in-hand with reality. In all the examples, it was assumed that there was a perfect world and that none of the factors which influenced a share's price altered. A general fall in the price of all shares naturally reduces the price of nil paid shares. A decline in the price of a company's fully paid shares has a greater proportional effect on the rights issue. Take the previous example of a 5-for-16 rights issue at 160p in Issue Right Limited. If the market price at the time of the announcement was 200p, the theoretical ex-rights price was 190.5p, in theory the value of each right was 30.4p. However, if the market price of the fully paid shares dropped to 180p, the theoretical ex-right price would be

$$175.2\text{p} \qquad \frac{(16 \times 180\text{p}) + (5 \times 160\text{p})}{21}$$

and in theory the value of each right would be

$$15.4\text{p} \qquad (180\text{p} - 175.2\text{p}) \times \frac{16}{5}$$

In other words, a 10 per cent fall in the price of the fully paid shares would result in a near 50 per cent fall in the value of the nil paid shares – in theory.

The price of rights is also subject to their own demand and supply. Not all shareholders will want to take up their rights. If the supply of rights to the market exceeds the demand, ie buying by other investors, the price of the rights will slip. Perhaps at a later date this situation will correct itself. The fact that the premium on nil paid shares falls is not in itself a reason for selling them.

Naturally, if a shareholding is small and the entitlement to subscribe for the new shares is likewise small, there can be situations in which they are not worth selling. The reason is that the commission a broker will charge for handling the sale transaction could well exceed the gross proceeds. In this situation, it is best to let the rights lapse.

Selling rights is an easy matter. Simply contact your broker or bank with your instructions. It will be necessary to forward the allotment letter completed and signed as indicated. The instructions are generally clearly presented. Remember that if you fail to act by the stated date, the rights lapse. Should you require guidance as to when to sell, for example immediately, or towards the end of the offer period, then seek guidance from your broker or financial adviser. As explained above, if there is heavy initial selling and no corresponding buying, the price can slip, but may well correct itself later. You can check the progress of your nil paid shares in the press.

Another course of action is to sell part of your rights and use the proceeds of the sale to pay for the shares that you take up. If you choose to do this, follow the instructions on the allotment letter. After the sale, you will receive a 'split' letter for the rights you have sold.

Consult your broker at the time of the sale to ensure that the closing date for the offer of the rights you have decided to take up is not missed. If the cheque for the rights you take up is not received by the closing date, of course the rights will lapse.

Buying rights

If a share price falls after a rights issue has been announced, investors who consider that the price will later recover can buy rights through a broker. Just as the fall of fully paid shares has a more marked effect on their nil paid counterparts, so does a rise. Those who wish to speculate can acquire rights in the hope that a small rise in the fully paid shares will be very profitable.

Underwriting

If a new or rights issue does not appeal to investors, does this mean that the company loses out? The answer is in the affirmative if the issue is not underwritten. This is a guarantee given by the 'issuing house' (generally a merchant bank or one or more stockbrokers) to take up the issue if investors do not. A fee is charged for the service. The majority of companies prefer their issues to be underwritten.

Scrip issues

Introduction

Commonly referred to as 'free shares' or a 'bonus issue', a scrip issue can be viewed as a nil priced rights issue. The exercise is nothing more than a bookkeeping transaction. Technically it is a capitalisation of reserves. When a limited company is formed its shareholders' funds are made up of its issued capital. Over the years, some of the company's profits are distributed to shareholders in the form of dividends, while others are ploughed back into the business. The bookkeeping procedure is to transfer the retained profits to reserves. The shareholders' funds therefore comprise the issued capital plus reserves. Providing all goes well, the reserves could exceed the nominal value of the issued capital. However, because the value of the company has increased, the price of the shares will bear no relation to their original issue price. Let us take an example, which, for the sake of clarity, considerably oversimplifies the situation.

Balance Sheet of Scrip Limited On Day One

	£		£
Issued share capital *(1 million £1 ordinary shares)*	1,000,000	Net assets	1,000,000
	£1,000,000		£1,000,000

Net assets per share £1

Let us assume that the company enjoys a prosperous ten years. After a decade its balance sheet could look like this:

Balance sheet of Scrip Limited ten years later

	£		£
Issued share capital *(1 million £1 ordinary shares)*	1,000,000	Net assets	10,000,000
Reserves	9,000,000		
	£10,000,000		£10,000,000

Net assets per share £10

If the company makes a 9-for-1 scrip issue, its balance sheet would look like this:

Balance sheet of Scrip Limited ten years later after 9-for-1 scrip

	£		£
Issued share capital *(10 million £1 ordinary shares)*	10,000,000	Net assets	10,000,000
	£10,000,000		£10,000,000

Net assets per share £1

Although the net assets per share have fallen from £10 to £1, the shareholder is in exactly the same position as before. This is because for every share that was held before the scrip issue, the shareholder now has 10. If the price of the shares on the stock market exactly reflected their net worth, it can be seen that the value of an individual's total holding is worth the same before and after the scrip issue. The 'theoretical' price of a share after a scrip issue is calculated exactly the same as for a rights issue (see Table

6.1). The 'issue price' is of course nil. Therefore, if a share stands at 200p before a 1-for-4 scrip issue, afterwards its price will be:

$$\frac{(4 \times 200p) + (1 \times 0p)}{5} = 160p$$

Why does a company have a scrip issue?

As a shareholder is in exactly the same position after a scrip issue as he was before, it may well be asked why a company bothers with such an exercise. The reason that is generally put forward by companies is that their shares are 'overpriced'. The view is expressed that if the unit price was reduced, more investors would become shareholders. In other words, a price of 900p may serve as a barrier to new shareholders, whereas they may buy at 300p. As £900 worth of shares either in the form of 100 at £9, or 300 at £3 is the same, this is baffling from the point of view of logic.

The psychological spin-off

Fact can be stranger than fiction and initially this appears to be the case with scrip issues. It cannot be denied that a scrip issue can increase the demand for a company's shares. However, there could be a logical explanation. Take our previous example of share at 200p before a 1-to-4 scrip issue. If the dividend was previously 8p a share, shareholders would receive 32p for every four shares held. After the issue, if the dividend was unaltered, shareholders would expect to receive 32p for every five shares held. However, this would be 6.33p per share. The demand for the shares may reflect the anticipation of the company increasing the dividend to at least 6.5p per share. In other words, the scrip issue could signal a dividend increase and hence a possible rise in the share price.

What is required of shareholders?

The brief answer to this question is 'Nothing'. Whereas action is required where rights issues are concerned, shareholders just sit back and let a scrip issue happen. The event will be reported in the press. Perhaps the issue will have to be approved by shareholders at the company's Annual General Meeting (AGM). The timetable for the issue may also appear in the press. Details will be sent to shareholders. One of the pertinent dates is the 'records date'. All those on the shareholder's register at that date are entitled to the scrip issue. Five to ten days afterwards, the shares will be quoted ex scrip in the market. As explained in Chapter 2, the letters 'xc' will appear after the price to signify the adjustment.

As soon as the new certificates are ready, they will be mailed to shareholders. Those wishing to sell their entire holding before their new certificate arrives, may still do so, for stockbrokers will be fully aware of the situation. For example, with a 1-for-1 scrip issue, the 'old' holding will be doubled to arrive at the 'holding' of 'new' shares. It must be made clear to the broker that you wish to sell x 'old' shares, which are equivalent to 2 × 'new' shares. When the new certificate arrives, it must be forwarded to the broker.

Other issues

Although the main situations regarding issues of shares have been dealt with above, others may also be encountered. These will now be examined briefly.

Loyalty shares

These are not to be confused with a scrip issue. A loyalty issue means that shareholders receive free shares, given in proportion to a holding at a particular moment in time. For example, founder shareholders in British Telecom received a 1-for-10 loyalty issue (based on their initial shareholding) three years after the company was privatised, provided that they still held their 'founder' shares!

Consolidation

This is like a reverse scrip issue and involves the 'writing-up' of a company's shares. For example, a company with ordinary shares with a par value of 5p, may decide to restructure their capital and have ordinary shares with a nominal value of 25p. Shareholders would therefore have their holdings reduced to one-fifth of the original, but the share price would increase by a multiple of five in compensation.

Sub-division

This is the reverse of a consolidation. For example, the nominal value of the shares being 'written-down' from £1 to 25p. This would quadruple a shareholder's holding, but quarter the value of each share.

Stock split
The US equivalent to a scrip issue. However, a 2:1 stock split is the same as a 1-for-1 scrip issue.

Scrip dividend
This is the issue of shares in lieu of a cash dividend. More companies are giving shareholders this choice. It is a method of increasing a holding without incurring dealing costs. The following shows the timetable for J Saville Gordon Group plc's scrip dividend alternative for its final dividend in 1989:

Monday, 14 August 1989	Ordinary shares quoted ex-dividend
Thursday, 24 August 1989	Record date for final dividend
Monday, 11 September 1989	Posting of forms of election
Monday, 2 October 1989	Final date for receipt of forms of election
Wednesday, 18 October 1989 (1030)	Annual General Meeting
Friday, 27 October 1989	Cash dividend paid
Monday, 30 October 1989	First day of dealings for new ordinary shares

7
Other Investments

'Money is a sixth sense which makes it possible for us to enjoy the other five'
Richard Ney

Introduction

Shares are not the only investments upon which the press report, neither are they the sole investment medium in which individuals can place their money. There are many ways in which funds can be put to work. Bank accounts and building society share accounts, National Savings Certificates, unit trusts, investment trusts, endowment policies, pension plans and Premium Savings Bonds are all possibilities. Perhaps you may wish to become 'a person of property' and buy a flat or house to rent to a tenant. Those with a penchant for the theatre may be tempted to become an 'angel' and put money into stage productions. Perhaps the thoughts of 'the Midas touch' may lure you towards gold. If the environment holds an interest, then perhaps investing in a Scottish forest may appeal. Connoisseurs of fine arts may buy pictures, silver or ceramics to enjoy, but also in the hope that their cherished objects may appreciate in value. Undoubtedly the most liquid of investments are fine wines and one of the most speculative, a share in a racehorse. Starting your own business is perhaps the greatest investment commitment you can make.

I am not suggesting that every newspaper covers every possible form of investment in its financial pages, but it is amazing how many areas *are* covered by financial journalists. Personal finance pages may cover investing in antiques or some other form of 'alternative investment' and give guidance to those contemplating buying a franchise. Articles may appear on your chances of winning a prize if you buy Premium Savings Bonds, or report on the experiences of those that have bought a share in a racehorse. Tables detailing last year's best performing unit trusts may be published, or the top interest rates for savers. The previous day's prices for bullion coins may be printed regularly and general advice given regarding pensions or personal taxation.

The objective of this chapter is to outline the purely financial information, other than details of shares, that you will find in the press on a daily basis. As the book is particularly for personal investors it will concentrate on gilts, investment trusts, unit trusts, insurance policies and pension plans linked to unit trusts.

Gilts

Introduction

One small investment adviser once advertised the investments upon which he was prepared to give advice. He mentioned endowment policies and pension plans, unit trusts and shares. He ended with 'Guilts'. Whether this was a Freudian slip, or a typographical error is not known, for he went out of business before enquiries could be made.

Gilt-edged, or more commonly 'gilts', is just a nickname for Government stocks. The certificates issued by the Bank of England on behalf of the Government are not, and never have been, edged with gold. More than likely the name derived from the fact that the interest rate is guaranteed by the Government.

Gilts provide the Government with long-term finance. The interest rate is not the only thing that is guaranteed. A feature of gilts today is that the stock will be redeemed at a specified future date. In other words, the original capital will be returned. There are a few 'undated' stocks quoted in the market. For example, there are the 2½ per cent Consolidated Stock (2½ per cent Consols) which were originally issued in 1883 to replace an 1855 stock. When gilts are offered for sale, the redemption date may be anything from 3 to 30 years away. However, holders can convert their stock into cash at any time by selling through the Stock Exchange.

It may be considered that gilts are a superb form of investment – they provide a regular income and the original capital is returned at a future date. However, there are dangers. Inflation eats into all fixed interest rate stocks as the purchasing power of the interest paid, as well as the real value of the capital, diminishes. Although index-linked gilt-edged stocks have been available to the private investor since 1982, ordinary gilts are not inflation-proof. As gilts can be bought and sold on the stock market, they can and indeed do fluctuate in price. So, although with redeemable stock, the Government guarantees to return

£100 of stock every £100 issued, it is possible to lose or make on gilt deals in the interim period. The prices of gilts are published daily in the national press.

Published prices of gilts

The *Financial Times* publishes just over 100 gilt prices. The other quality papers publish a similar number. Whereas shares are divided into different sectors, ordinary gilts are categorised as to their redemption date. 'Shorts' have lives up to 5 years, 'mediums' from 5 to 15 years and 'longs' over 15 years. 'Undated' and 'index-linked' gilts have separate categories of their own. The prices are found at the beginning of the share price page. For example, in the *Financial Times*, 'British Funds', as gilts are officially known, are found at the beginning of its 'London Share Service'. Incidentally, please note that the FT's Share Service begins on the page before the double page spread of prices.

We will now examine the information found in the *Financial Times*.

High–Low

As with share prices, the first column gives the high and low figures of a particular gilt for the year, or the last year plus the current year to date. The period to which the figures relate is given at the top of the column, eg 1989 or 1989–90, etc.

Stock

To help differentiate between the gilts, they are given different names such as Conversion, Exchequer, Funding and Treasury. Some are referred to as 'Stocks' while others are 'Loans'. Here are a few examples:

Treasury 13 per cent   1990
Exchequer 12½ per cent 1994
Conversion 10 per cent   1996
Funding 3½ per cent   1999–2004

Obviously the papers use abbreviations such as Treas.13pc. The name of the gilt is academic. What is important is the percentage rate (known as the 'coupon' rate) and the redemption date. When two redemption dates are given, eg 2012/15 the Government can redeem the stock at any time from 2012 to 2015. The actual date it chooses will depend on the level of interest rates generally. If they fall below the coupon rate, it may pay the

Government to redeem the rates as quickly as possible. The reverse is the case if the coupon rate is below the general prevailing rate. A symbol after the name of the stock indicates that upon application interest can be paid tax free to non-residents of the UK. Otherwise, interest is paid with basic rate tax deducted. (Note: Interest on gilts purchased via the National Savings Stock Register is paid without deduction of income tax – see page 136.)

Price
The price quoted is the 'middle price', ie the figure falling between the *offer* and *bid*, at the close of business the previous working day. The 'spread' between offer and bid prices is small. Do remember that, as with shares, the price of gilts will fluctuate throughout the day. Prices are always given for a £100 nominal value of stock. Fractions and not decimals are quoted for part of a pound.

+ or –
This shows the price change on the previous day's close. Changes are quoted in terms of £1. Naturally $^{8}/_{32}$ is quoted as ¼, etc. On Monday, this column is omitted and semi-annual interest payment dates inserted.

Yield int.
Nor surprisingly, the yield interest (also called the 'running' of 'flat' yield) is the one that is most significant to the majority of investors. Indeed, professionals refer to yields as opposed to prices. It is the interest yield that a holder of the stock will receive at the market price. Mathematically it may be expressed as:

$$\frac{\text{Coupon Rate}}{\text{Market Price of £100 Nominal Value of the Stock}} \times 100$$

Yield interest is quoted gross.

Yield red.
The yield to redemption is the total return to an investor if the stock is held to maturity. In other words, it is the aggregate of all gross interests dividends and the capital gain or loss at redemption annualised. If a stock is bought at £80, there will be a tax-free capital gain of £20 at redemption. If stock is purchased at £110, there will be a £10 capital loss when it matures. If there is going to be a gain, the yield to redemption will be higher than the

interest yield and vice versa. An extract from the British Funds section will illustrate this point:

		Yield	
Stock	**Price (£)**	**Int**	**Red**
Treas 8 pc 1993	91½	9.01	11.31
Treas 13¾ pc 1993	108 9/16	12.66	11.08

Undated gilts
The published information is as for dated gilts, but there is obviously no yield to redemption. There are only half a dozen undated stocks.

Index-linked gilts
Index-linked gilts are inflation-proof in two ways. The dividend is raised every six months in line with the Retail Price Index (RPI). At redemption, the original capital is repaid in real terms. However, the nominal value of the stock does not increase in line with inflation. The indexing of the capital repayment is undertaken at redemption. Index-linked gilts are traded on the market just like ordinary Government stock. In other words, they fluctuate in value as other stocks and shares.

		Index-linked				
1989/90		**Stock**	**Price**	**+/or**	**(1)**	**(2)**
High	**Low**					
112¾	103 7/16	Tr 2pc '92 = (97.8)	111 13/16	− ¼	3.50	4.63
105 9/16	94 27/32	Do 2 pc '94 = (102.9)	104¾	− ¼	3.16	3.72

Financial Times, 18 January 1990

The price information given in the papers follows the usual format – High-Low, name of stock, price and the change on previous day's close. However, the yield columns differ. Both show prospective real redemption rates, but at different projections of inflation. The chosen inflation projections are 5 and 10 per cent respectively. There is also additional information in the stock column. Figures appear in parenthesis. These are the RPI bases upon which the sum paid at redemption will be based. It may appear confusing that the bases are below 100. This is because the RPI was rebased in January 1987 to 100. The figures have been adjusted to reflect rebasing.

Ordinary gilts and the investor
The price of ordinary gilts is inversely related to the general

interest rate prevailing in the market. In other words, when interest rates rise, the prices of gilts fall. Gilts are always quoted per £100 nominal value. In the stock description column, the name of each gilt includes a 'coupon' rate of interest. This is the rate at which the Government will pay interest on each £100 nominal value of the stock. Therefore, in the case of a fictitious undated Treasury 10 per cent stock, a holder with a nominal value of £100 would receive £10 interest each year. When the general interest rate in the market is 10 per cent, it is reasonable to assume that this stock will sell at £100 per £100 nominal value. However, would this be the case if interest rates generally were 5 per cent?

The answer to this is 'No'. The coupon rate does not vary throughout the life of a gilt-edged stock. The only variable is its price in the market. In theory, if the interest rate generally prevailing in the market halved, other things being equal, the price of gilts would double. Take our example of the imaginary undated Treasury 10 per cent stock. If the general interest rate in the market fell to 5 per cent, in theory, the price of the stock in the market would rise to £200 as this is the sum investors would be required to invest at 5 per cent to obtain a return of £10. If the general interest rate in the market were to double to 20 per cent, in theory the price of our fictitious undated Treasury 10 per cent stock would halve to £50, the reason being that this would be the sum required to produce an income of £10. To summarise:

£200 @ 5 per cent = £10
£100 @ 10 per cent = £10
£50 @ 20 per cent = £10

In theory, the price of the stock in the market would inversely reflect rises and falls in the general rate of interest prevailing. However, this oversimplifies the matter. Just glancing at the High-Low prices in the press will reveal that gilts fluctuate in a small band. Most gilts are dated, ie will be redeemed at their nominal value at a specified future date or during a certain period of time in the future. Assume that the Treasury 10 per cent stock in our example was not undated, but was redeemable a few years hence. At such time, holders with a nominal value of £100 of the stock would receive £100 at the redemption date. Consequently, it is the yield to redemption that will be of interest. This factor is therefore one of the determinants of price in the market. As with everything quoted on the stock market, the price of gilts is also subject to the laws of supply and demand.

It is important to remember that with the exception of index-linked gilts, gilts are 'fixed interest' securities – the amount of income you receive each year does not change, whatever happens to interest rates in general. Gilt-edged prices and interest rates tend to balance at opposite ends of a see-saw. When interest rates fall, gilt prices in the market rise.

Buying gilts

Gilts can be bought and sold through a stockbroker. The dealing costs are lower than for purchasing equities (say, 1 per cent against 1.95 per cent). Although there are no transfer duties as with shares, the stockbroker's minimum commission charge must be remembered.

It may be considered prudent to delay buying gilts until just before the half-yearly interest is due to be paid in the belief that there will be an added bonus of nearly six months' interest receivable on the holding. Unfortunately, it does not work like this. The proportion of the interest due to the buyer and the seller is worked out on a daily basis at the time of the deal. The appropriate amount of 'accrued interest' is added on or subtracted from the consideration as appropriate. The calculation is shown on the contract date. An example for buying £1000 Treasury 10 per cent 1994, when 90 days' interest has accrued, would read:

£1000 10 per cent Treasury Stock 1994 @ 94	£940
Plus 90 days' accrued interest	25
	£965

Of course, there would also be the broker's commission. At the half-year interest payment, the stockholder would receive an interest cheque for £50. The seller would receive consideration for the stock with accrued interest added. In other words, buyers 'purchase' their portion of interest accrued since the last interest payment, while buyers receive it for the period they held the stock.

(Note: Accrued interest is gross and has to be accounted for on an annual tax return. Settlement for gilt transactions are on a cash basis within 48 hours of the deal. No capital gains tax is payable on profits as a result of a sale or the receipt of redemption moneys. On the other hand, there is no capital gains tax relief for losses.)

New issues

Until the mid-1980s new issues of gilts were regular events. They still occur, albeit not as frequently as in the past. Keep an eye out in the financial press for details. Anyone can apply for stock in multiples of £100. Incidentally, it is not always issued at par (ie £100) but more often than not at a discount (say, £95). This does not mean that you get something for nothing. The combination of the coupon rate and the redemption date means that the Government is not paying over the odds for its money. However, it cannot be denied that some issues are more attractive than others. The prospectus will state the terms of the offer. There are three possible ways of offering the stock:

- at a fixed price, the total sum payable being required at the date of application;
- as above, but only part payment being required immediately, with the balance becoming payable in two instalments at later dates;
- by tender with an initial payment, the balance being paid in two instalments.

New issues for gilts follow the basic procedure for new issues of shares outlined in Chapter 6.

National Savings Register

With the increase in stockbrokers' minimum commissions, small shareholders are somewhat disadvantaged for their dealing costs are spread over a small value holding. Their unit cost is therefore proportionately higher than for a larger investor who enjoys the economies of scale. Whereas there is little an investor can do with regard to purchasing existing shares quoted on the stock market, it is different where gilts are concerned.

The Department of National Savings operates the National Savings Stock Register. A leaflet giving full details is available from main post offices. Basically it is a 'gilts by post' service. The scheme has several advantages. Foremost it is at an extremely competitive cost. In June 1990, the following commission charges applied:

Purchases

Cost of transaction	Commission charged
Not exceeding £250	£1
Over £250	£1 and a further 50p for every additional £125 (or part)

Sales

Proceeds of sale	Commission charges
Less than £100	10p for every £10 (or part)
£100–£250	£1
Over £250	£1 and a further 50p for every additional £125 (or part)

Furthermore, interest is paid gross. There are disadvantages, but these are not too burdensome. The Director of Savings cannot undertake to buy or sell securities at any specified price, or on any particular day. However, purchases and sales are always transacted as soon as practicable. Although the full range of gilts cannot be dealt with through the Register, a reasonable selection is available. Full details are contained in the leaflet. 'Buy' and 'Sell' forms, together with post-paid envelopes are available from main post offices.

'Buy' or 'Invest'?

If you are buying 500 shares in a company there can be no grounds for confusion. Your broker is simply instructed to buy 500 shares on your behalf. With gilts there are two possible lines of action – buying or investing.

Needless to say, it is essential that you make it perfectly clear which you are doing.

Buy

This means that you instruct your broker (or the Director of Savings) to buy £1000 nominal value of a particular stock. If it is quoted below £100, you will pay less than £1000 and vice versa (plus commission).

Invest

This means that you buy stock so that its cost and commission does not exceed a certain sum, say, £1000. If the stock is quoted below £100, more than £1000 nominal value will be received and vice versa.

Other fixed interest stock

Gilts are not the only fixed interest stocks available to investors. Immediately below its prices of British Funds, the *Financial Times* lists a selection of loan stocks. There are corporation loans, ie stock issued by city and local authorities, as well as building societies, international bank and overseas, Commonwealth and African loans and foreign bonds and rails. The information presented is exactly the same as for gilts. In certain situations, the return may be higher than for gilts. However, remember that loan stocks do not have the backing of the British Government.

Companies also issue fixed loan stocks. Debentures and secured loans are secured on property owned by the company. Investors therefore have a safety net if the company fails – provided of course that the value of the security adequately covers the total nominal value of the debentures issued. Holders of ordinary loan stock do not have the advantage of a safety net in the event of a company going into liquidation. Investing in unsecured loan stock may well pay a higher interest than gilts – the margin above the return of gilts reflects the market's consideration of the extra risk involved. It is naturally important only to purchase unsecured loan stock in healthy companies and where the interest payments are adequately covered by profits. Debentures, secured and unsecured loans are quoted underneath the price of a company's ordinary shares.

Unit Trusts

Introduction

Unit trusts invest in shares quoted on the world's stock markets. When an investor buys units in a unit trust, he is buying a stake in the unit trust's total shareholding. One of the main advantages of this form of investment is that it is a way to reduce the risks generally involved when buying shares. 'Don't put all your eggs in one basket,' is a common expression. Unit trusts follow this advice. Typically a unit trust will buy shares in 50 to 100 different companies. Therefore they are an inexpensive and convenient way for investors to spread their risk. The average small investor will not be in a position to buy decent holdings in up to 100 companies. An investment of, say, £10,000 in 100 different shares would mean a holding of about £70 in each company if minimum dealing costs were £30. Administering such a portfolio would be burdensome. Dealing with rights and scrip issues, dividend cheques and completing the annual tax return would be a Herculean task.

The purchase of a unit trust alleviates such problems. The management of a unit trust's 'portfolio' is undertaken by professional fund managers. They decide which shares to sell and which to add to the trust's shareholding so as to strive to achieve the objectives of either income or growth, or a balanced combination of the two. Naturally, a unit trust will only perform as well or as badly as the shares in which the fund managers invest. It is important to remember that although unit trusts spread the risk of stock market investment, they do not eliminate the possibility of losing money. As the value of the underlying shares fluctuates, so too does the price of units.

Naturally the unit trust managers do not operate their investment schemes for nothing. They make their profits and cover their expenses in two ways. The first is the 'initial charge'. This is around 5 to 6 per cent and is the difference between the 'offer' price (the price at which the investor buys units) and the 'bid' price (the price at which the investor sells units back to the unit trust managers). In addition, there is an annual management charge which is levied half yearly. This varies from ¾ to 1½ per cent of the total value of the fund. Generally it is deducted from the income earned by the trust (eg dividends and interests received) before the distribution to unit trust holders.

There are over 1200 UK unit trusts from which to choose. They are divided into 15 broad categories.

- *UK General Trusts.* These provide a broadly based investment in mainly UK shares, covering several industries. The aim of such trusts is steady growth in both income and capital values.
- *UK Growth Trusts.* The emphasis here is on a rising unit price rather than the payment of high income. Within this category you will find specialist unit trusts, like those which invest entirely in the shares of small companies or in recovery stocks.
- *UK Equity Income Trusts.* The priority of these trusts is to provide investors with an above average and growing income from the ordinary shares of companies. Many of the trusts also have a good record of increasing investors' capital.
- *UK Mixed Income Trusts.* Unit trusts investing in both shares and fixed income investments which aim to produce high income.
- *Gilt and Fixed Interest Trusts.* Funds investing in Government securities and corporate bonds. With 'income' gilt and fixed interest trusts, the provision of a high and secure income is the main consideration, while with the 'growth' gilt and fixed interest funds the concentration is on capital appreciation.

- *International Growth Trusts.* While rather similar in nature to UK general trusts, these funds spread their investments throughout several different world stock markets. This limits the risk to investors of putting all their eggs into one stock market basket.
- *International Income Trusts.* Some overseas income trusts invest in a broad spread of international markets, while others concentrate exclusively on America, Japan, Europe or the Far East. All the funds are designed to provide an above average income, as well as some capital appreciation, from portfolios of overseas stocks, shares and bonds.
- *North American Growth Trust.* These invest in American and Canadian companies. Some trusts offer a general spread of shares, while others invest in more specialised areas like smaller companies, recovery stocks or companies concerned with new technological developments.
- *European Growth Trusts.* Most of these funds invest in the shares of companies in a number of different European countries. However, there are also trusts within this category which concentrate exclusively on French, German, Spanish or Scandinavian shares.
- *Far Eastern Growth Trusts.* Investment can either be in a spread of companies in Japan, Hong Kong, Malaysia, Singapore, Australia and New Zealand, or it can be concentrated in individual stock markets in the region, like Hong Kong, Singapore or Malaysia.
- *Japanese Growth Trusts.* The majority of the portfolios will be invested in Japan, either in a general spread of shares or in specific sectors of the Japanese market like smaller companies, technology stocks and recovery situations.
- *Australia Growth Trusts.* These invest in a spread of Australian companies and occasionally in British companies whose interests are mainly in Australasia.
- *Financial and Property Trusts.* These provide an investment in the shares of financial institutions like banks or insurance companies and in the shares of property companies.
- *Commodity and Energy Trusts.* Investment here is concentrated on the shares of companies producing raw materials, oils and other commodities such as gold and other precious metals.
- *Investment Trust Units.* Trusts investing in the shares of investment trust companies. Investment trusts themselves invest in a wide range of companies.

There are two further types of fund.

- *Fund of Funds*. These are either unit trusts which invest exclusively in at least four other unit trusts in the same group, or a new type of fund which invests in a range of other unit trusts, not necessarily managed by the same group.
- *Money Market Funds*. These invest in cash, such as bank accounts and wholesale money market investments. Their principal use will be to provide a haven for investors who wish to be temporarily out of stocks and shares. They do not offer 'capital certainty' as do ordinary deposit accounts.

Unit trust prices

The *Financial Times'* 'Unit Trust Information Service' spreads over nearly three pages against just over two for its 'London Share Price Service'. The *Daily Telegraph* and *The Independent* devote as much space, if not slightly more, to unit trust prices compared to share prices. *The Times* coverage is not so comprehensive, whereas the *Guardian* does not report unit trust prices at all.

It is usual for newspapers to group all the unit trusts from each unit trust manager together. The groups of unit trusts themselves fall under three main headings – authorised, insurances (or insurance and property bonds) and offshore and overseas. An authorised unit trust will have been approved by the Securities and Investment Board (SIB) under the Financial Services Act. Only authorised unit trusts can be advertised and be offered for sale to the public. Insurances will be dealt with later, but in brief they relate to unit linked endowment policies or pension plans. Offshore and overseas unit trusts fall into two categories – those recognised and unrecognised by SIB.

Authorised UK unit trusts are subject to strict controls. There are obligations to make full particulars available, controls over the permissible underlying assets as well as over the pricing of units and other aspects of the management of such schemes. Recognised overseas schemes are also subject to strict regulation, but in the country in which they are based. Overseas schemes are only 'recognised' by SIB if the rules of their regulatory authorities satisfy its standards. In contrast, unrecognised schemes may not be subject to such controls. There may be no obligation to make particulars available; no control over investment or borrowing powers, or the pricing of units. Consequently, investors may not be able to redeem units at their net asset value. In other words, there could be a hefty penalty for realising such an investment. It is therefore important to appreciate the differences between authorised, recognised and unrecognised unit trusts.

The amount of information on unit trusts given from one newspaper to another varies. The most comprehensive is the *Financial Times'* 'Unit Trust Information Service'. Here is what it reveals:

- *Managers:* The full names and addresses of the unit trust managers are given, together with telephone numbers for enquiries and dealing.
- *Funds:* The names of the funds are given in abbreviated form. Accumulation units, where the income is automatically reinvested in the trust (after payment of basic rate tax) are either indicated by the letters *Acc* or *Accum Units*. If the latter appears in brackets under the name of a fund, the first line relates to distribution (ie income) units in the fund, the second line to accumulation units in the same fund.
- *Time:* The time shown by the fund manager's name is the time at which the unit trusts' daily dealing prices are normally set, unless another time is indicated by an individual unit trust name. Each company decides at what time of the day it reprices its funds.
- *Init. Chrge:* The initial charge represents the marketing, administrative and other costs which have to be paid by new purchasers. It is included in the price when the customer buys units.
- *Canc. Price:* The cancellation price is the lowest figure allowed by SIB for the repurchase of units. The figure varies with the net asset value of the fund. The maximum spread between the offer and bid price (see 'Price') is determined by a formula laid down by the Government. In practice, unit trust managers rarely use the maximum spread allowed, but are content with a narrower spread. Consequently, the bid price is often set well above the minimum permissable price, or cancellation price. Usually investors can sell their units at the bid price, but when there is a lot of selling (eg when the stock market generally declines sharply), this may be lowered to the cancellation price. If the bid price and cancellation price are close or identical, it generally means that there are probably more investors selling than buying that particular unit trust.

- *Price:* Two prices are always quoted for unit trusts. The lower one is the *bid* price. This is the figure which investors receive when they sell their units. The higher of the two prices is the *offer* price. This is the figure which investors pay when they purchase units in the trust. Note that there is no separate commission when buying or selling unit trusts. The dealing costs are built into the offer and bid prices. For example, the offer price is made up of the cost of the underlying shares represented by a unit, dealing expenses and the initial charge the unit trust company makes for managing the fund on behalf of investors.

The *spread* is the difference between the bid and offer prices. The SIB can allow a spread of up to 11 per cent. However, the industry's norm is usually in the region of 6 per cent.

Since July 1988, unit trust managers have used three different methods of pricing their units:

- historic;
- forward; and
- historic and forward.

The historic basis values units in a fund at the previous day's prices of the underlying shares. Consequently, investors may deal at the prices quoted in today's newspaper (which quotes the previous day's prices) *provided* first, that there has not been a revaluation of the fund since the figures were supplied to the newspaper and second, that the managers have not switched to the forward pricing basis. The *Financial Times* indicates an historical pricing basis by the letter *H* after the time which appears immediately following the name of the unit trust company.

As the name implies, the forward pricing basis values the underlying shares at a future date. Investors dealing on forward prices will not know the exact price at which they have bought or sold until later, as the price will be set at the next regular revaluation after they have dealt. The *Financial Times* indicates a forward pricing basis by the letter *F* after the time which appears immediately following the name of the unit trust company. When prices are quoted on a forward basis in a newspaper, they are the price at which investors dealt on the previous working day.

Some unit trust companies use a combination of historical and forward pricing. The actual basis used depends on the time of the day that an order is processed. For example, an historic basis may be used for deals up until noon and forward pricing thereafter. The scheme particulars, which are available free of charge from unit trust companies, will fully outline the pricing basis used. Some companies only revalue their funds weekly or fortnightly.

- *xd:* Ex-dividend indicates that new unit holders are not entitled to the recently declared dividend.
- +/−: The price movement reveals how the offer price has moved since its last quotation in the paper.
- *Yield Grs:* This is the estimated annual distribution before tax, expressed as a percentage of the quoted offer price.

(Note: The above information is the maximum information that appears in the authorised unit trust section of the *Financial Times'* 'Unit Trust Information Service'. The insurance and part of the offshore and overseas sections are not so detailed. Other newspapers report varying degrees of unit trust details.)

Which unit trust to choose?
One of the problems with unit trusts is that there are so many from which to choose. The various categories have already been outlined. The 'Fund of Funds' or UK General Trusts could be the answer for first-time investors. Of course, investors can be more adventurous as there is certainly a large variety of funds from which to choose. It is all a question of personal choice and the risk you are prepared to take. For example, unit trusts which invest overseas fluctuate in value, not just because of the performance of the underlying shares, but as a result of exchange rates varying. Reading the financial press can assist in decisions as to which category of unit trust may be advantageous for investment. For example, reports that the economies of Thailand and Singapore are booming may make unit trusts which invest in those areas attractive. A general common-sense interpretation of the effect of current affairs, news stories and industry reports on the financial markets can also be beneficial.

However, having decided in which general category to invest, how do you decide on a specific unit trust? Performance tables are published in the personal finance press as well as from time to time in the personal finance pages of the national press. The tables can cover various periods from a month up to 15 years. A comparison over a one- to five-year period will generally be adequate. Although it may be tempting to pick the fund at the top of the latest table, and be influenced in your decision-making by its consistently good performance. A unit trust that is always in the top quarter of a table is far sounder than one that appears at the top once and thereafter is in the third division. Do remember that past performance is not necessarily an indication of the future.

As well as publishing performance tables from time to time, the financial press also comment on categories of unit trusts. For example, as independent taxation approached, features appeared on money market funds. Although unit trust distributions are paid net of basic rate tax, the tax payment is recoverable from the Inland Revenue. The funds therefore became attractive to married women who were not taking advantage of their tax allowances. Similarly, if it is reported that a particular geographical area is prospering, articles may appear analysing the funds that invest in the countries within that region. However, perhaps the greatest coverage is given to launches of new unit trusts. The merits or otherwise of the new units is analysed in varying degrees of depth. A similarity between the features indicates that the journalist is relying heavily on material supplied by the unit trust managers. Do not just look at the traditional financial press. Stockbrokers' newsletters are another good source of information which may assist your decision-making process. If making a choice is all too much, guidance can be bought from an independent adviser.

It is worth noting that the Unit Trust Association publishes regular statistics on the performance of the middle-performing funds in each category. These figures are available free of charge from:

The Unit Trust Association
65 Kingsway
London WC2B 6TD

An 8½in × 4in stamped-addressed envelope must accompany your request.

Buying units
There are two basic routes for buying unit trusts:

- direct from the managers; or
- through a financial adviser.

Incidentally, it is traditional to invest a certain sum of money in a unit trust – the minimum sum is generally £500 – as opposed to buying a specific number of units. Let us now examine the two ways of making a purchase.

Dealing direct

The telephone number and address of the unit trust managers can be found on the unit trust prices pages of quality newspapers at the head of the group of units they manage. A couple of days after the purchase you will receive a contract note recording the transaction. As unit trust purchases are 'cash deals' you will have to forward your cheque when the contract note arrives. A few weeks later you will receive your certificate.

When a new unit trust is launched, there is usually an extensive advertising campaign. Most of the adverts incorporate an application form. Very often for an initial period, the managers offer a discount to 'founder' unit holders. These vary from 1 to 3 per cent of the offer price.

Buying through an adviser

Financial advisers fall into two categories and it is important to appreciate the difference between them. A company representative is a tied agent and will only offer 'best' advice on the range of unit trusts offered by a particular unit trust management company. In other words, the advice will be limited to the units within a particular investment stable. An independent adviser is exactly what the title suggests and his 'best advice' will embrace all unit trusts. Under the Financial Services Act 1986, an adviser is obliged to indicate whether he is a company representative or independent at the beginning of a consultation.

In certain instances, for example a 'cold call' from a doorstep salesman, the Act gives the investor a 14-day 'cooling-off period' in which to change his or her mind. However, this is not an opportunity to monitor the price of the units and decide to bow out of the deal if values fall, for any drop in the price during a cooling-off period has to be borne by the investor. The period begins when you receive a cancellation notice advising you of the 14 days in which you may change your mind.

Share exchange schemes

Some unit trust companies offer share exchange schemes. These are useful for investors with several small shareholdings who wish to move from direct participation in the Stock Exchange to unit trusts. Eligibility for the schemes depends on the shares held and the size of the portfolio. Details are available from the managers. Generally, if the shares are acceptable to the managers, they may be taken into the trusts under management at the prevailing offer price. The investor could also save on dealing costs. Possibly unacceptable holdings will be sold at an advantageous rate of commission.

Regular savings schemes

An alternative to a lump sum investment in unit trusts is a regular savings scheme. This can be a very good introduction to indirect stock market investments. Regular commitments start from £20 per month.

Apart from committing capital out of income, the schemes can also have another advantage for investors. It is known as 'pound-cost-averaging'. It works like this. If over the period of saving the price of units declines, then your regular sum saved will buy more units. The reverse is the case when the price rises. Provided the market fluctuates over the saving period, you will always have paid a lower average unit price than the market average over the same time-scale. Of course, this will only benefit investors who sell their units when the price has risen.

Some unit trust companies offer loyalty discounts for savers who have participated in such a scheme for a certain period. Note that a regular savings scheme is not a contractual commitment for a specific length of time. It may be cancelled at any time. Should your holding be valued below a certain level you may have to sell your units.

Selling units

Should you decide you want 'out' of a particular category of unit trust, it is usually possible to switch to another fund managed by the same company at a discount.

Selling all or part of your holding is a simple matter. Contact the managers direct by telephone or by letter. The addresses and dealing telephone number(s) are given in the press. It will be necessary to return your certificate with the renunciation section on the reverse completed. Sellers are normally in receipt of their proceeds within five working days of the managers receiving the renounced certificate.

Investment Trusts

Introduction

'When is a trust not a trust?' This question is not as frivolous as it may appear. The answer is 'When it is an investment trust'. The fact is that investment trusts are not trusts at all. They are in fact limited companies which are quoted on the Stock Exchange. Their business is not manufacturing, retailing or the provision of services, but holding shares. While there are similarities with unit trusts – for example, apart from the obvious one that both hold stocks and shares, neither pays capital gains tax on share dealings – the two are quite different animals. A share in an investment trust is determined by the law of supply and demand and consequently its price may bear no relationship to its underlying net asset value as its shares are traded on the stock exchange like any other company's shares. On the other hand, units in a unit trust are bought and sold by the unit trust company's managers at prices extremely close to the net asset value of each unit. An investment trust can have a rights issue or raise more money by issuing a loan stock. Both of these fund-raising vehicles are denied unit trusts.

Investment trusts were formulated in the nineteenth century as a means of raising venture capital for pioneering investments overseas. Over the years their investment outlook changed and they concentrated on forming portfolios of shares quoted on the world's stock markets. Therefore, many now have an international flavour.

The price of investment trust shares

When the City analyses an investment trust, there is a yardstick that it views with interest. This is the trust's net asset value (NAV). It is the market value of the trust's share portfolio less its liabilities, such as loan stocks and any preference shares that the trust has issued. The NAV is on a per share basis. The *Daily Telegraph* publishes investment trusts' NAVs on a daily basis. The Association of Investment Trust Companies publishes a monthly information booklet listing each of its member's NAVs.

The comparison of NAVs and investment trust share prices is interesting as the latter are nearly always below their NAVs. The fact is that investment trust shares generally trade at a discount to their NAV. The average discount at the end of 1989 was in the mid-teens with general investment trusts trading at 18 per cent below NAV and growth and Far East trusts at about 10 per cent. However, certain investment trusts with portfolios of European equities were trading at a premium over NAV. Interestingly, the average discount to NAV in the 1970s reached 45 per cent. However, throughout the 1980s, the discount has been slowly narrowing.

The discount to NAV of course is a result of an investment trust's share price and is not a determinant of the price. However, as we will see, a high discount can stimulate demand and thus move a trust's share price upwards. There are numerous reasons why a particular investment trust is considered desirable. If a trust's share portfolio performs well, the increase in the value of the underlying shares, other things being equal, will result in investors wishing to share some of the good fortune. This will especially be the case if the prospects for the future are also expected to improve. For example, a weak pound will make trusts with overseas holdings appealing. If the geographic region in which the majority of the fund is invested is enjoying an economic boom, this will increase the demand for the shares. As long as demand exceeds supply, the share price of the trusts will increase. Of course, the reverse will have the opposite effect. The poor performance of a trust, adverse exchange rates and a poor economic outlook in the geographic area in which a trust has the greatest exposure will all have negative influences on its share price.

Mention has already been made of the discount stimulating interest in a particular investment trust's shares. This will occur when the shares are trading at a high discount to the trust's NAV. Predators may be lured to a trust in the hope of 'unlocking' the assets. For example, the British Coal Pension Fund, in a search for a cheap portfolio, took over TR Industrial and General, the flagship of the Touche Remnant stable – such a takeover should benefit shareholders in the trust. Another tactic design to decrease the discount margin is to unitise the trust. However, this does not always work. Shareholders are offered units in a unit trust or offshore collective investment fund in the hope the units will trade at or near the NAV of the original portfolio.

One reason for the reduction of discounts in recent years is the return of the private investor. In the 1970s, it appeared that small investors had abandoned investment trusts in favour of unit trusts. However, possibly as a result of an ongoing public relations exercise by the Association of Investment Trust Companies, such fears proved unfounded. Even so, about 75 per cent of the total of investment trust shares are owned by the institutions – insurance companies and pension funds, etc. Institutional investors tend to favour specialist as opposed to general trusts on the basis that the former may invest in areas where they do not undertake research. It is believed that a good proportion of institutions would dispose of their general investment trust holdings if share prices approached NAVs. If this was to happen, the shares in general trusts could fall in value. It is a point worth bearing in mind.

Split capital investment trusts
Reference has already been made to the specialised investment trusts whose portfolios are invested in particular geographical areas. There is nothing special about the format of such trusts, but this is not the case with split capital investment trusts. Their construction is totally different from the normal run-of-the-mill trust. They were originally devised with the objective of eliminating discounts on NAVs. Two classes of share are issued – growth and income. The former receive any of the capital appreciation achieved by the shares in the portfolio, whereas the income shares receive all the dividends. It is not just the split aspect that makes these investment trusts special. At a predetermined future date, the trust is liquidated. According to the terms of the trust the income shareholders may receive a proportion of the value of the portfolio or nothing at all. The capital shareholders, who have not enjoyed any income during the period they were shareholders, will receive the bulk of the portfolio. Hopefully they will receive a sizeable capital gain for their patience.

Certainly, the shares in investment trusts with a life of 10 to 15 years are priced at a substantial discount to the portfolio's NAV. Income shares can produce an above average and increasing return, but, when the trust is liquidated income shareholders receive either a small proportion of the portfolio's value or nothing at all. However, the total income over a 10- to 15-year period could be very attractive. Certain brokers have an expertise in investment trusts and their advice should be sought regarding the suitability of split capital investment trusts. Some split trusts offer more than one class of share in order to offer permutations of capital and income shares. Others include warrants and zero dividend preference shares.

Unit linked investments
In recent years unit linked investments have become increasingly

popular. An endowment policy, pension plan or investment bond may not initially appear to have much in common. However, if they are unit linked there is a common theme – the investment vehicle for all of them is unit trusts. If there is a life cover element in the investment, for example, it is an investment bond or endowment policy, the units will be listed under insurances. Units relating to pension plans may be found either under authorised trusts or insurances. The progress of units can be followed in the national press. Where lump sum investments are concerned, you will be told how many units in a particular fund have been acquired shortly after the transaction has been finalised. Where regular payments are made, investors are sent periodic statements advising of the number of units held.

It was not until January 1990 that the exact size of the life office's involvement with unit trusts was known. The following extract from *The Independent* is interesting as it not only reveals the value of the insurance companies' holdings of unit trusts, but gives the paper's view of the new tax treatment of unrealised capital gains in the funds. This is a good example of how investors can obtain views of investment schemes generally.

Granted a lease of life

The mass withdrawal of holdings by life offices in unit trusts seems to have been headed of by publication of phasing-in arrangements for the new tax treatment of unrealised capital gains made on the units.

The Unit Trust Association yesterday revealed that life insurance companies hold 45 per cent of funds held in unit trusts.

The news that insurance companies have such a dominant position does not come as a surprise, but it is the first time the information has been released.

At the end of 1988 the Unit Trust Association and Bank of England estimated that life insurance companies held units worth £18.6bn out of a total of £41.6bn. The value of the unit trusts at the end of 1989 rose to £56.1bn . . . .

The precise effects of the tax changes will differ, depending on the investment policy of the life company and specifically how fast they turn over their portfolios. The impact will also differ on units held for endowment policies compared with unit-linked contracts.

The effect on the latter will be to reduce the maturity value of the average unit linked policy by an estimated 1 per cent.

For the small investor this simply makes the unit-linked life policy route into unit trusts even more unattractive than before.

The Independent, 25 January 1990

8

Information and Records

News has a short shelf life Harford Thomas

It goes without saying that shareholders like to follow the progress of their shares. The real enthusiast will chart the price of individual shares on a daily basis. From time to time, the financial press publishes graphs of a company's share performance over a period. Certainly, charts and graphs show you the history of movements of share prices at a glance. Chartists are technical analysts who plot the patterns of trading so as to help them forecast future price movements. They are great devotees of the use of graphs. However, this is a complex subject and out of the scope of this book.

Nevertheless, it is essential for even the smallest of shareholders to keep some records of their portfolio. At some future date the price you paid for a particular holding may be required for capital gains tax purposes. For this reason, Contract Notes relating to purchases and sales should all be kept.

Of course, where new issues and rights issues are concerned, there are no Contract Notes. As it is so easy to forget how much you paid for a certain holding at a later date, it is prudent to record the details at the time the shares are acquired. How this is done is a matter of personal choice.

You may prefer a note book or a loose-leaf file. Another possibility is a small card index system. This method has the advantage of being compact and flexible. What information should you record? Here are a few suggestions:

- date of purchase;
- number of shares acquired;
- price per share;
- total consideration;
- price per share inclusive of commission;
- FT-SE 100 Index on the day of purchase;

153

- FT-Actuaries Share Indices on the day of purchase, eg the sub-section in which the share is placed (ie chemicals, stores, etc), or the All-Share Index.

The reason for including the indices is that the progress of the share price can be monitored against the sector and the market generally. It is far easier to record this information at the time of your purchase than to try and ascertain past indices at a future date. If your shares perform better than the market you have good reason to be pleased with your share choice and vice versa.

By adding details of rights issues, scrip issues and scrip dividends, you will have an up-to-date record of your holding as well as its history in chronological sequence. However, you will also want to monitor the progress of your total shareholdings as well as the individual shares which make up your portfolio. A table can be constructed listing all your shares which includes the net and gross share price and the total consideration paid for each holding. Periodically, you can value the portfolio and ascertain the percentage increase, or decrease, against its total cost. When these valuations are undertaken, the main indices can be recorded so that you can judge your performance as a fund manager.

A share certificate may just be a piece of paper, but it does represent your share in a company's business. Some investors take a very paternalistic interest in the enterprise they part own and attend shareholders meetings and even correspond with the managing director about certain issues. Others are quite content to just follow the price of their shares and to read the press comment. Share ownership can be turned into a hobby. It can be fascinating to follow a company's progress over time and it is very easy to start a file on a company in which you have an interest. It is also quite surprising how quickly the files can grow in certain instances, particularly if your interest is in one of the larger companies which attract the most press coverage.

By filing press cuttings you can build up an interesting dossier on a company. Perhaps it may just be a brief mention in a market report, the reporting of an acquisition or disposal, a comment made by the chairman or an in-depth article. However, taken as a whole, they provide a fascinating insight into the company. This approach, which does require self-discipline in monitoring the press and taking the trouble of cutting, mounting and filing the newspaper or magazine clipping, is an excellent way of focusing your mind on your holding. What you read may give you great encouragement. On the other hand, it may signal the fact that it is time to sell certain shares and to look for another investment that may be more attractive.

There is no reason why you should restrict this operation to the companies in which you have a financial interest. It is a fact of life that you may not have the money to invest when you read of a fantastic tip for a particular share. Do not despair. In the majority of cases, the tipping of a share raises the price (market makers *do* take note of tipsters' comments and anticipate the increased demand by moving their prices upwards). If you do not have funds available, monitor the share's progress. Start a cuttings file on the company and keep the investment opportunity in mind for when you have spare cash. If you still consider the shares a viable proposition at a later date, when you have funds, it could well be that the shares can be purchased at a lower price than at the time that the tip was published. Alternatively, you may conclude that the investment was of a speculative nature and that events have not materialised as the tipster anticipated. In such cases, you will have side-stepped a capital loss. Should the shares have soared, you may have 'missed the boat'. That is life and there is no point in becoming depressed about lost opportunities.

In addition to compiling files on individual companies, you could also collect cuttings about sectors that would be useful background material. For example, you may decide to keep a file on the retail sector, or breweries and distillers. These can be used in different ways. For example, if you hold shares in Marks & Spencer, this would supplement your company file. Should you decide at some stage that you are disappointed with the performance of your M & S shares, it may help you to choose another retailer which may have more potential. On the other hand, if you have no brewery shares but decide that you would like to diversify into this sector, the file could provide useful background material to assist you in your decision.

Should you purchase a new issue, it would be prudent to retain a copy of the prospectus in your company file. This document will contain a host of material about the company. It will outline its past history and give its plans for the future. At a later date, it will be interesting to compare its actual achievements with past objectives. A company's annual report and accounts can also be filed. Needless to say, from time to time you will have to have a weeding-out session, or you may find that you have a storage problem!

There may be occasions when you want information about a company which your own files do not reveal. City institutions take advantage of the statistical services provided by such companies as Datastream, Extel Financial and Micropal, but individual shareholders will usually find that the services specialist companies are too expensive. Your own stockbroker may be willing to assist, depending upon your rapport with the member of the stockbroking firm's staff with whom you deal and their workload at the time.

Information on companies and sectors on the stock market can also be obtained from MacCarthy Cards, which are published by MacCarthy Information Limited of Manor House, Ash Walk, Warminster, Wiltshire BA12 8DY (telephone 0985 215151).

The library supplying this information goes back some 20 years, and covers all companies which are quoted on the Stock Exchange, both on the London Exchange and provincial exchanges. Also covered are the companies quoted on the USM, Third Market and 8000 unquoted companies. Information can also be obtained on European and Australian top companies.

Investors can either write or telephone to obtain information. Costs vary according to the information required; for example, regular weekly information on a minimum of five companies will cost £19.50 (plus VAT) per week per company, while information on a particular sector of the market, say industry, will cost £81 per annum plus VAT.

You can undertake your own research. This is easier if you have access to a good business library. By referring to the company cards produced by Extel Financial you can glean a host of information. The annual cards contain details of the business, subsidiary and associated companies; an analysis of profits for 10 years or more; dividend details; share earnings; summary balance sheets for two years; net asset value per share; share high and low prices over a period of years; gross yields and PE ratios at a range of prices, together with a synopsis of the chairman's statement. News cards covering interim reports and developments since the last annual card are issued periodically. Institutions and stockbrokers subscribe to the full service. Perhaps your own stockbroker will give you sight of the cards of the companies which interest you if you do not have access to a business library. Individual cards can be purchased from Extel at a cost of £14 per company. For this fee, the annual card and most recent news cards are forwarded. Extel may be contacted on 071-253 3400.

Sources of historical information

Handbooks are useful sources of information. Some are published quarterly, others every six months, while others still appear annually. A popular one is *The Hambro Company Guide*. It appears quarterly and the current annual subscription is £69.50. Published by Hemmington Scott (071-278 7769), it has become recognised as one of the leading providers of business information. The publishers describe the *Guide* as, 'an information service on the UK Corporate Sector for use by businessmen, bankers, advisers and investors'. Comprising over 750 pages, it contains a wealth of information. All UK companies with equity shares fully listed on the Stock Exchange, together with companies whose shares are dealt in on the USM, Third Market or Over the Counter, together with certain companies which have raised capital under the Business Expansion Scheme, have entries. Data is given for a five-year period and includes turnover, pre-tax profits, earnings per share, dividend per share, fixed asset, fixed investments, stocks, debtors, cash and market capitalisation – in other words, short form profit and loss and balance sheet information. Gearing ratios (the percentage of debt capital to equity capital) and return on capital employed are given where appropriate. Most entries include a share price graph which also shows how the share price has performed in relation to the FT All-Share Index.

Hemmington Scott also publish *The Hambro Performance Rankings Guide* which evaluates the financial performance of over 2000 UK fully listed companies. Performance is ranked on 22 different counts and there are also comparative league tables based on 27 different criteria. Two editions are published each year and the current annual subscription price is £135. As good as these guides are, they are probably too comprehensive for the average small investor. Although not expensive in relation to the information they contain, purchasing your own copies would not be cost-effective.

The Unit Trust Year Book is the essential reference for the unit trust enthusiast. It does not restrict itself to statistical data. The first section is devoted to commentary and reference. It even covers basics. For example, 'What is A Unit Trust?' is the title of one of the articles in the 1989 *Year Book*. However, the impression must not be given that this is a beginner's guide. The publication covers over 150 management groups and over 1322 authorised unit trust funds. There is a review of the previous year and comments on the performances achieved. Practical advice is given on choosing a unit trust, where to obtain advice and how to invest. The second section is devoted entirely to statistics. There are performance tables for growth and income, unit trusts are listed by size and monthly sales are also detailed. Almost every statistic that could possibly be of interest is recorded. The final section is devoted to management groups and unit trust details. The latter covers all authorised unit trusts. Apart from all the information you would expect to find, for example, the type of fund, minimum investments, the portfolio distribution, charges and yield at the end of the previous year, there is also a tabular record of the trust. High-Low figures are given for 10 years, as indeed is the income distribution. *The Unit Trust Year Book* is the official year book of the Unit Trust Association and is published by FT Business Information Limited in co-operation with the Association. It appears in April each year and is updated in the autumn at £45. As with *The Hambro Company Guide,* investors may find it more cost-effective to consult rather than purchase a copy of the *Year Book.*

The Association of Investment Trust Companies publishes an annual *Investment Trust Directory* which will be a useful reference source for investors interested in investment trusts.

APPENDIX
How to Buy and Sell Shares

In order to buy and sell shares you require the services of a stock-broker. Since Big Bang investors can deal direct with market-makers (prior to October 1986 their function was undertaken by jobbers), but their contact is with institutions and private investors wishing to transact large volumes of shares. Although there have been mergers of broking firms in recent years, there are still a large number from which to make your choice. Recently banks and building societies have also established stockbroking functions. The Stock Exchange publishes the *Private Investor's Directory*, a booklet listing stockbrokers who are interested in providing services to private investors. This is obtainable from the Stock Exchange in London and from its regional offices:

Irish
- The Stock Exchange, 28 Anglesea Street, Dublin 2
  Telephone: 0001 778808

Midlands and Western
- The Stock Exchange, Margaret Street, Birmingham B3 3JL
- The Stock Exchange, Share Information Centre,
  Birmingham International Central Concourse,
  Birmingham B40 1PA
  Telephone: 021-780 4213
- The Stock Exchange, St Nicholas Street, Bristol BS1 1TH
  Telephone: 0272 264541

Northern
- The Stock Exchange, 76 King Street, Manchester M2 4NH
  Telephone: 061-833 0931
- The Stock Exchange, Royal Exchange House, City Square,
  Leeds LS1 5SG
  Telephone: 0532 451511

- The Stock Exchange, Silkhouse Court, Tithebarn Street, Liverpool, L2 2LT
  Telephone: 051-236 0869
- The Stock Exchange, Commercial Union House, 39 Pilgrim Street, Newcastle upon Tyne NE1 6RJ
  Telephone: 091-232 7355

Northern Ireland
- The Stock Exchange, Northern Bank House, 10 High Street, Belfast BT1 2BP
  Telephone: 0232 321094

Provincial
- The Stock Exchange, London EC2N 1HP
  Telephone: 071-588 2355

Scottish
- Stock Exchange House, PO Box 141, Glasgow G2 1BU
  Telephone: 041-222 7060
- The Stock Exchange, 91 George Street, Edinburgh EH2 3ES
  Telephone: 031-220 1684

Having secured your *Directory* you should select several stockbrokers who look as if they may suit your needs and either arrange to call and see them, or, if they are some distance from your home, chat to them by telephone. There is no need to deal with one in your geographical region, but naturally your telephone bill will be smaller if you do not decide to opt for 'long distance' dealing!

It is important to establish each broker's scale of charges. Although there may not be much to choose between the commission percentage, it is crucial to establish the minimum commission. Some brokers may have a minimum charge of £20, others £30 or £40, while some of the more prestigious firms may levy a minimum fee of £50 or more per transaction. At the end of the day, the cost of dealing on the Stock Exchange is of importance. A typical scale of commission for equities, preference shares and convertible stocks is as follows:

	Consideration
1.95% up to	£7000
0.70% on next	£8000
0.60% on next	£115,000
(thereafter by negotiation)	

If you are contemplating holdings where the consideration will be £1500 or less, it makes sound economic sense to opt for a broker who has a low minimum commission. For example, at 1.95 per cent the commission for buying shares valued at £1000 will be £19.50. If the minimum commission is £20, there is an 'excess' charge of a mere 50 pence. However, with a minimum fee of £30, this rises to £10.50.

Stockbrokers offer three kinds of service:

Dealing only: Also known as 'execution only', it is as the name implies, a basic dealing service. Advice is not a part of this service.

Advisory: This is the basic 'execution only' service enhanced by the broker playing an advisory role when requested by his client. The Financial Services Act 1986 requires brokers to give 'best advice' in relation to an individual investor's circumstances and the level of risk he is prepared to take. Consequently, clients requiring an 'advisory' service will be requested to complete a 'Know your Customer' questionnaire. Please note that 'best advice' is not synonymous with 'best investment' – it is purely an opinion as to what is best.

Discretionary: This is a service which brokers offer 'high net worth' clients, ie those with a substantial portfolio. The investor gives the broker absolute discretion to deal with the shares with the object of achieving agreed objectives of maximising either growth or income, or a combination of the two.

It must be remembered, however, that the cost of dealing within a particular firm does not vary according to which category of service the client chooses.

With high minimum commissions, it appears that some brokers are going out of their way to discourage investors with small investments. Thankfully, others do not wish to see those with small shareholdings become an extinct species and offer a 'no frills' execution service only.

Periodically, the personal finance pages of newspapers and magazines, such as the *Investors Chronicle*, give details of conventional brokers and share dealing services which offer investors a good deal. If you require a straightforward dealing only service, using those that offer economically priced buy or sell transactions makes sound sense.

The services fall into three categories: a 'face-to-face' situation, telephone transactions or a postal service. An example of the first are share shops. Some are located in department stores, others in banks, whereas others have their own premises. An example of a telephone service is *Sharelink*. Full details may be obtained by telephoning 021-200 2242. Occasionally newspapers run a special offer whereby readers may sell specific shares by post.

It is worth researching to see what is currently on offer. At the time of privatisation issues or large flotations on the stock market, special offers for selling shares abound. It is financially prudent to take advantage of such 'square deals'.

Index